NAKED

NAKED

on sex, work,
and other burlesques

essays by

FANCY FEAST

ALGONQUIN BOOKS
OF CHAPEL HILL   2023

Published by
ALGONQUIN BOOKS OF CHAPEL HILL
Post Office Box 2225
Chapel Hill, North Carolina 27515-2225

an imprint of WORKMAN PUBLISHING CO., INC.,
a subsidiary of
Hachette Book Group, Inc.
1290 Avenue of the Americas
New York, NY 10104

Printed in the United States of America.
Design by Steve Godwin.

Library of Congress Cataloging-in-Publication Data

Names: Feast, Fancy, [date]– author.
Title: Naked : on sex, work, and other burlesques / essays by Fancy Feast.
Description: First edition. | Chapel Hill, North Carolina : Algonquin Books of Chapel
    Hill, 2023. | Summary: "Burlesque performer, sex educator, and social worker Fancy
    Feast gives readers a backstage pass to the nightlife and sex industries, examining
    our culture's hang-ups and obsessions with bodies, desire, and even love"
    — Provided by publisher.
Identifiers: LCCN 2023021019 | ISBN 9781643752372 (trade paperback) |
    ISBN 9781643755427 (ebook)
Subjects: LCSH: Feast, Fancy, [date]– | Stripteasers—United States—Biography. |
    Sex—United States. | Sex industry—United States.
Classification: LCC PN1949.S7 F43 2023 | DDC 792.7092 #a B—dc23/eng/20230612
LC record available at https://lccn.loc.gov/2023021019

10 9 8 7 6 5 4 3 2 1
First Edition

To the fats and femmes before me,
and to the fats and femmes after

Two or three things I know for sure, and one is that I'd rather go naked than wear the coat the world has made for me.

—Dorothy Allison

CONTENTS

· ·

NAKED

The Assorted Nudities

. . . .

I'm going to open my dress for you, just a little, because I'm nice, and because when I do, we will both get something out of it. I am the one on stage undressing, but I am not revealing myself to you. Rather, you are revealing yourself to me. In the milky glow of reflected stage light, I am observing your face and how it changes, whether I can provoke your surprise or catch you in a private moment that no one but me gets to witness. The fourth wall is flimsy; nevertheless you lean against it like it will not fall away, and I can see pleasure and bewilderment splashed across your face in momentary bursts, the wonderment of your mouth, which has fallen open; the shame and embarrassment that knits your brows together and prompts you to cast down your gaze to your hands to examine the folded gum wrapper there; the laughter that bursts forth from you like rain dropping from a cloud in humid spring. Hi baby. Thanks so much for coming to the show. It looks like you're having fun.

I'm the one taking off my clothes, but in these moments you are more naked than I am. Make no mistake: you are not the voyeur you imagine yourself to be, secreted away and safe in the audience of a darkened theater, in the back row of folding chairs in a sweaty, beer-soaked bar. You feel safe because I am the show and you paid to see it. What you don't realize is that you and I are here for the same reason: because we like to watch. The difference is, I know you're watching me.

You have no idea that when I strip for you, we each face a reflective surface.

I'm a burlesque performer. I've been nestled in this humid corner of the New York City nightlife scene for a decade now, the seedy underbelly of a recently pitted and sanitized metropolis, performing feats of nudity for audiences enraptured and stultified alike. It's a living; half of one, anyway. Burlesque in New York is a writhing, roiling industry and a cultural center for burlesque communities around the world, a who's who of nightlife infamy, and an engine of innovation, driven by fickle audience preferences and performer ingenuity. Jaded, seen-it-all-before city dwellers pour into our bars and clubs and back rooms on evenings and weekends, wasted and loud, and it's my job to show them something they can't see anywhere else. It takes something extra to rise above the din in a town where even the squirrels are so embarrassed with choice that they have preferences for name-brand nuts over inferior deli almonds. Although New York City boasts some of the smallest, grungiest burlesque venues in the world, it is populated by more headliners per square inch than anywhere else. What it lacks in hospitality, it makes up for in frequency of bookings, because the city's population gets bored, needs novelty, and works too hard not to play a bit. If you're decently talented, and sometimes even if you're not, you'll work a lot here. There is a burlesque show somewhere in the city every night of the week; all you need is to know where to look and to bring a handful of cash.

When I tell people that I do burlesque, I think they imagine me wearing little top hats, crinoline skirts and ruffle butt panties, striped stockings, a . . . what? A cane? Sorry to disappoint, but this isn't an old-timey Wild West photo op, and I'm not a fucking saloon girl. Sure, I've got sequined gowns and feather fans and headdresses that set me back a grand or so, and sometimes I'll even perform to a jazz standard or a big band song, but I'm using the comforting grammar of glamorous womanhood to plant an explosive in your evening, and at some point, I'm going to detonate it. If I am doing my job right, something I do in my act will surprise you, disquiet you, linger after my final reveal is once again obscured by curtains. Burlesque as an art form burrows under the skin like a parasite, feeding off your blood and enthusiasm. If you take a regular ant and expose it to a specific kind of fungus, the fungus hijacks the brain of the insect, turning the ant into a zombie and feeding off its internal energy stores while the fungal growth gains power, eventually bursting out of the ant's head and raining down spores to pass into the body of a new target. If you've seen me at one a.m. on a weeknight hand-applying three-millimeter rhinestones one at a time onto the planetary surface of a 38FF bra, in repeating patterns, destroying my grip strength and my retinas in the process, you know that the burlesque fungus has taken me over and has got me fucked up beyond any hope for recuperation. If you've seen me perform and you're still thinking about what you saw, the spores have replicated. I'm toast, and you're about to be, too.

Burlesque took over my brain early. When I was fifteen, in tenth grade, my high school put on *Cabaret* as the big winter musical. I was originally cast as Fraulein Schneider, the old German landlady. It was a juicy role but I didn't want it. The role of the old, sexless crone or pathetic undesirable always, *always* goes to the fat girl. If Juliet needs a nurse, if any ingenue needs a mom or grandma, or if, God forbid, your high school puts on Neil LaBute's *Fat Pig*—those are the roles to which fat girls are relegated. I could not and would not tolerate it. David, my high school crush (also one of my best friends—hey, it was high school) was going to be in the audience one of those nights. I wanted him to see me dolled up and languid. Maybe I could seduce him with the raw sensuality of a high school musical chair dance, in my matte black, one-inch character shoes. Though it would be a smaller part, I asked the director to cast me as a Kit Kat Girl, and like that, I joined the chorus line as Frenchie.

The mothers who volunteered as costume assistants for the show were flummoxed when tasked with outfitting my body, which was and is best served by plus sizes. They handed me maximal undergarments, items requiring an augmentative modifier, not so much lingerie as *lingerissimo*. Sad, modest fat girl items from brands named after real or imagined zaftig wearers: Karen Woman, Barbara Intimates, Linda: Private Label. While the other girls got fishnets, I wore black control top pantyhose. I pleaded with the mothers to let me wear something sheer on top so I would be visible from the stage, and when they reluctantly relented, I tried on my first ever piece of lingerie—a black, empire-waist slip with floral embroidery—in front of a bunch of moms in a fluorescent-lit high school auditorium. Wearing it, I felt infinite.

Frenchie wasn't just any old factory-floor-model chorus girl. In my hands, Frenchie was blasé, a good-time girl with no good times to be had. She'd known bad men and had been fucked around, used, and discarded. Frenchie wore wet burgundy lipstick and fingerless gloves, and I even asked the backstage makeup artist to draw track marks on Frenchie's arm and hickeys on her neck. I borrowed a cigarette from a senior boy in the cast and pressed it onto my lower lip so it hung listlessly from my mouth. Frenchie had lived and loved and seen the worst the Weimar era had to show her, or so she thought.

In reality, I was an insecure virgin performing a chair routine for my fellow students and their parents in an all-purpose room with a green rubber floor. But for a couple of hours a night and one Sunday matinee, I was a tragic, disaffected, sexy French girl with haunted eyes who danced for money and the attention of the patrons at the Kit Kat Club. And as I stared out into the audience, I could for the first time see the reactions I got by putting myself on lascivious display. My teachers and the PTA were not the ideal target demographic, but still, I got high on the feeling and never wanted to leave the stage. When the show closed, I rummaged through the Theater Department's costume closet after school and stole the black slip. It's still hanging in my closet.

In the summer after my freshman year of college, my cool older friend Sarah Marie invited me to sleep on her couch when I visited New York, so that I could accompany her to see a scripted striptease theatrical called *Pinchbottom*. My stomach clenched and I was suddenly nervous, as if I were going to perform myself, but I said yes and felt worried that none of my clothes were cool enough. We sat in the second row of crappy folding chairs at a downtown black box theater called Collective:Unconscious, a nonprofit that opened in a condemned brothel in the Lower East Side and closed thirteen years later due to an irreconcilable sewage situation. In the years between its birth and death, it produced some of the most sublime, absurd, experimental theater in the city; there, the fantasies of artistic freedom pressed against the limitations of reality like faces against a closed glass storefront. The space was shabby. The floor was in need of a good mopping, and you could make out the brushstrokes in the black paint on the walls. But at showtime, in the right lighting, the real world around me disappeared, just like in the all-purpose auditorium room at my high school. With the stage illuminated, the theater dark, and the audience murmuring like hens settling in for the night, there was nothing to do but begin. The first stripteaser stepped on stage wearing red and gold fringe, tossing her thick hair, toying with her beaded opera-length gloves, removing her clothing in lockstep with the tempo of the music. Her gyrations were hypnotic. She swiveled her hips, the soft parts of her body jiggling with her shimmies. The audience hooted and clapped with the removal of each garment. I compacted the paper program into a wrinkled ball in my sweaty, grasping fist, which had been marked with a Sharpie X because I was underage. My folding chair had become a cannon, and I had been loaded into it like a fearless carnie and launched toward my fate. The Kit Kat Klub I'd dreamed of existed. It had been open and operating this whole time, while I sketched fishnetted figures in the margins of my high school planner. I gasped and whooped in the audience like I'd stuck my head out a car window and couldn't catch my breath in the rushing wind. Glamorous, sexy people lived in New York City, entertaining crowds with their wits and their bodies, and it was satirical and sincere, old world and new, gritty and transcendent. God help me, I was going to become one of them. Nuns are called to serve Christ and I was called to serve burlesque.

From then on, I spent my school holidays on Sarah Marie's couch, seeing as much burlesque as I could. I learned that when done correctly, a striptease employs the same rhythm—the same movements, notes, and rests—as a magic trick. Through artful direction and misdirection, your gaze is guided exactly where intended, for instance, toward the crotch right before the tearaway panties burst open to reveal a yet-tinier G-string, your gaze pulled away from the hands that grasp for the findings of a brastrap closure. Sometimes, even though I had been doing nothing but watching someone strip, I found myself surprised at the end of an act to see the performer was naked. A striptease doesn't land without rising tension, just as a magician doesn't just flop a dove out of his coat first thing. Instead, you are first asked to contemplate his gesture, his empty suit jacket, which makes the appearance of the bird a marvel.

That's why I laugh now whenever I hear someone in the audience yell at me to "take it off!" As if I'm not going to. As if doing it faster would be preferable. As if I could drop trou and spend two verses, choruses, and a bridge winking my asshole at a satisfied crowd. Maybe you think you want that, but I promise you don't. The internet is full of naked people these days, their outsides and insides. An unclothed body itself is not so rarified. It's my job to get you to lean forward in anticipation, to confirm or flout your expectations for what will happen next. The *what* is inevitable; the *how* is ineffable.

The idea behind my very first proto-burlesque performance was the reality of fucking all day, something I, at that point, had never experienced. I had two days to put together the choreography, with the two years I had spent watching people strip as my guiding force. My friend Lirael was putting together a show as a last-minute addition to her queer nightlife event, Shimmer, which took place at the rinky-dink bar on my college campus. The acts she'd booked were drag and lip-syncing numbers, and as we walked out of French class together, she asked me if I wanted to perform. The night of the show, I practiced my newly choreographed moves in the cold, cavernous downstairs bathroom of my decrepit off-campus house. I left improv practice early with my costume in a backpack. I dressed for my big debut in the echoey all-gender bathroom in the student union building. I didn't own any makeup. Lirael lent me neon pink lipstick and electric blue eyeshadow she'd shoplifted from the five and dime in town. I was shaking with the intensity of the adrenaline, so she had to help me apply it in exaggerated swooshes, shapes more feminine than my own face.

The song I chose was an R. Kelly song, "Echo,"* an ode to male sexual stamina. My choreography began with excitement

---

* I don't perform to this song anymore, for obvious reasons.

and arousal, which I staged as a sensual chair dance, echoes of my *Cabaret* choreography. As the song continued and the sex marathon went on, my spirits flagged. I winced from chafing and succumbed to boredom, reaching for my phone to text as I danced. As the song wound down, I stumbled, unable to stand, and as the music faded, I planned to crawl off the stage chugging a bottle of Gatorade.

I wanted to strip in the act, but I was too self-conscious. I didn't want people looking at my naked body. Sex and nudity were something I did off campus, with older men I was never going to see again. The stakes felt too high for someone to encounter me there, naked, and then later, clothed, as my whole pedestrian self. So I would hit my starting pose swaddled in a long-sleeved bathrobe and planned to crawl off stage in a short, tight black minidress concealed under it. Suddenly, the lights in the room shifted, bathing me in pinks and ambers and darkening the banal materiality of the space and the liberal arts students congregating within it. My nerves lifted me, and I danced as if I were on the tail of a kite. As I crawled off stage, I heard the sound of the applause, the roaring of an ocean, bouncing off the walls of the subterranean nightclub. That week I was a star on campus, with strangers approaching me in the dining hall to congratulate me. Someone posted on the anonymous online confession board that they had a friend crush on me. I'd kept my clothes on, but I'd revealed something about myself that people were excited to see.

After college I moved to New York, a stranger to almost everyone, which meant I was ready to transform into someone else, a cooler, more punk version of me, the kind of person who wanted her whole body on view.

We talk about nudity like it's a discrete and fixed thing with presence or absence—you're naked or you're not—but not the panoply of nudities, the intentional and inadvertent ways we reveal ourselves to one another. There are so many different ways to get naked. In my favorite burlesque acts, the act of getting undressed facilitates some other kind of revelation or transformation. Ms. Tickle, for example, strips away layers of a feather costume so she can construct long, elaborate wings out of them during her act, the unfurling of which creates the final tableau. Nyx Nocturne performs as a priest mid-sermon and, over the course of the act, strips so they can engage in ecstatic self-flagellation. Nudity doesn't need a reason to be present in a burlesque act, of course; it's an expected convention. But when it's used to further a narrative, it can be immensely satisfying storytelling.

Some nudity is political. Mine certainly is, whether or not I want it to be. Even if I create an act as a bird, as a tree, most people will only take away that I am fat, and therefore brave to strip in public. Bodies like mine are not often displayed in public forums as anything other than loci for abjection and ridicule, as "Before" pictures in weight loss ads. Maybe mine is the first fat body that my audience has ever seen unclothed in person, displayed for their gaze on purpose without shame or apology. Whether they're shocked, disgusted, aroused, angered, or excited by the sight of me, their reaction undresses them, not me. It is in the gasps or applause or silence after the final reveal that I can hear whether I have stripped the audience bare.

For others, nudity is a punchline. Lucida Sans, producer of the Rhinestone Gorilla burlesque troupe, describes her group's nudity this way: it's like the anarchic glee of a naked toddler running around the house after a bath. Each reveal of flesh or undergarment is an opportunity for a laugh. To be naked and laughed at is not a liability for them but the point. The troupe treats sexiness as incidental, secondary to, say, spitting out teeth as the climax of a striptease taking place during the portrayal of a stress dream. *If you're turned on by it*, their acts seem to suggest, *that's on you.*

Then there's nudity that's stark, dramatic, even grotesque— acts where the final reveal discomfits the viewer, implicates their gaze. Deity Delgado is known for this kind of thing, whether she's doing the act where she begins with her head fully bandaged and ends bald and grinning through tape that distorts her features into a facsimile of botched plastic surgery, or her intense, personal abortion piece, where she acts out self-terminating her pregnancy and eats the gelatinous fetus she passes. You don't know if you should be cheering when you see tits in a number like that—and listening to the room make that decision one way or another is part of the act itself. Her work is slow and deliberate as she ratchets up the tension, unrelenting. People freak out! People demand refunds! It's fantastic to watch.

Conversely, nudity can act as a painkiller. Backstage one night, Jo "Boobs" Weldon, the headmistress of the New York School of Burlesque, told me that she knows that she isn't the most flexible contortionist or the most amazing dancer. "But," she told me before I protested in her defense, "I have this thing where I can make people forget about the sadness in their lives, even if just for a few minutes." She's right. When Jo is on stage, some people in the crowd go slack while others stiffen, but no one looks away or checks their phone. She holds them all, dilating time with her presence. Nothing hurts when you're watching Jo, unless she wants it to.

On my way toward what counts as nudity, I can make myself look more expensive than a dead-eyed finance bro or his camel-coated girlfriend using only the contents of a beat-up carry-on suitcase my mom bought me at Marshalls. The illusion works, and so most people imagine that burlesque's luminaries are being chauffeured to gigs in a limousine, or that they can use their wages to afford luxuries like housing or health care. I can slink around on stage like I'm the wealthiest, fanciest, upper-crustiest gal and then grab some halal-cart takeaway and take the subway home at the end of the night. Burlesque is art that, often, encourages the audience to forget that we are artists, living on artists' wages unless bankrolled by a spouse, generational wealth, or a day job. It is class drag. And because people buy into this particular cultural story, they tend to feel more respectable attending a burlesque show than visiting a strip club. This assessment is faulty, not to mention whorephobic, and it underlines the strained puritanical relationship Americans have with the intersection between sex and money. Oftentimes, I hear people say that burlesque is feminist or retro or artistic expression, probably because it's not lucrative. American culture hates it when people financially benefit from sexualized labor. Women especially are expected to offer this kind of flirtatious attention and service, this kind of exaggerated gender perfor-mance, for free. Burlesque as a form of work is often perceived as a nonfunctional and artistic hobby. Stripping at a club will generally earn you more than burlesque, however, which intensifies the hatred for people working at strip clubs. But burlesque gets to be quirky, talked about as the kind of thing a woman does "for fun," and therefore performers can still wear the mantle of "empowerment" in the public eye. Of course I believe this is all bullshit, but that doesn't matter. When I've taken off my costume at the end of my number, I'm still wearing those projections.

In my lifetime so far, the dominant cultural pendulum has swung away from freedom of sexual expression. Despite the population becoming more liberal overall, there has been a proliferation of political initiatives limiting and legislating sexuality, from school boards banning books that mention the mere existence of queer and trans people to the (sweepingly bipartisan) passage of the disastrous SESTA/FOSTA bill in 2018. This law makes third-party websites legally responsible for anything that happens on their platforms that could be perceived as facilitating sex trafficking, resulting in sex workers losing the ability to advertise and screen for safety. It has also reduced free speech protections, which has increased targeted digital censorship of queer people and educational materials about sexuality. In its wake, the world is less safe for people working in the sex industry. Sex sells, as the adage goes, but you can't find it in app stores or on most major social media outlets, especially if you're fat or trans or trying to earn money with nude images, because your body is perceived as more obscene than others. Sex sells until the payment processer or credit card company you rely on decides that you're an undesirable party that no longer fits their corporate image and so you get banned or booted, locked out of your account, your assets frozen. Sex sells, but maybe not enough to gain access to a pension or health insurance. Sex sells, but not if the sex you're selling is your own.

These changes have been swift and galling. I've been working in the sex industry for more than a decade now, as an entertainer, as a sex educator, and more, and I'm lucky to have established my career before this latest wave of conservatism. The veneer of respectability that burlesque carries, along with my own unearned privilege, has shielded me from the worst our culture has to offer to people working in the sex industry. I was fortunate enough to be able to choose my niche and not get punished too much for it. So far, at least.

Down here, in the borderlands between virtue and vice, consumers are not so careful about what parts of themselves slip out. I get to learn about what people desire, what they fear, how they treat people like me, and who they believe themselves to be. Because I work in a place where people expose their secret wishes and unconscious desires to me, I've constructed some elaborate masks I wear to keep myself safe—to give people what feels like nudity but isn't, what feels like vulnerability but isn't. But these masks are heavy, hard to breathe in, and sometimes I want to take them all off. Do you want to see me take them off?

There. I see you and you see me. So let's be naked together for a bit, in one way or another, because when it's done right, it reveals something about us all.

Dildo Lady

· ·

After eight hours of near-constant touching by several hundred New Yorkers, the lips of the Fleshlight classic, a vulva-shaped masturbation sleeve made of a porous material called cyberskin, will begin to resemble the lint trap of a washing machine. Gray pilling accrues in the divot of the perfectly symmetrical labia. Stray human and cat hairs stretch like tightropes over the precipice of the vaginal opening.

I had perfected the process for cleaning the floor model Fleshlight. First, I spritzed the surface of the vulva with toy cleaner until it had a dewy sheen, like it had just emerged from a yoga class. I applied a fresh paper towel to it and pressed it on like a mask, tracing its creases. I slowly removed the paper towel like one of those blackhead strips, pulling up layers of gunk. Spritz, press, peel, until the vulva was once again soft artificial pink and shining. Then I wrenched the guts of it from its black plastic container so I could turn it inside out and rinse it. When I removed the sleeve from its sheath it made an audible, suction-y complaint, the unpursing of lips. As a child, I read a book of folklore from around the world. The tale that has stayed with me is about the Penanggalan, a Malaysian cryptid, a not-quite-woman who at night detaches from her body and flies through the air, just a head and spine with entrails dangling, attacking pregnant women and newborn infants. Whenever the wobbling cylinder of the Fleshlight was wrested loose for cleaning, it was the Penanggalan I pictured, feeling the night air against her insides.

I wasn't the only one mythmaking with the sex toys. They have a tendency to take on a kind of supernatural significance as talismans for good and evil. Sex toys are inanimate but intimate, personal but abstracted and inert. People imbue them with hopes, fantasies, and inadequacies. For seven years, I sold them.

I worked at a sex toy store, one of a dozen jobs I applied to when I moved to New York after college. I got turned down for a media job after pitching a piece about an erotic bakery. The nonprofit where I was interning didn't have enough money to hire me. The comedy theater didn't return my calls for a front desk position. The comic book shop wasn't interested. Only two places called me back: the sex shop and a ghost tour company, and the sex shop called first. Despite my having quit years ago, there are things that will cling forever to the terrain of my cerebral cortex, and how to clean a dirty Fleshlight is one of them. Shake me awake in the middle of the night tonight with a butt plug in each hand and ask me to compare and contrast them for you, and I could do it, no problem. On my deathbed, ask me about the composition of semen. Hold a mirror to my mouth to see if I'm still alive and I will breathe quiet condensation onto its surface. *Mostly . . . water. Fructose. Amino acids.*

•••

What was your sex education like? What did you learn, and from where? Did you get the talk on a car ride with your dad, unable to tuck and roll out of the back seat because the child locks were on? Did you get separated by gender in a middle school health class for a lecture on pregnancy from your gym teacher? Did a member of your church press clear tape to the skin of each of your classmates until it no longer adhered and then tell you to limit your sexual activity or else you'd never be able to connect with someone else? According to the Guttmacher Institute, only thirteen states require sex ed curricula to be medically accurate, which is, scientifically speaking, fucking wild. While eighteen states and Washington, DC, require that school-based sex ed programs provide information about contraception to students, twenty-seven states require that abstinence be the focus of the curriculum, despite numerous longitudinal studies that show that teens who get abstinence education have higher levels of STI transmission and pregnancy than teens who receive comprehensive sex ed. In some cases, abstinence education is worse than doing nothing at all because of the way the curriculum promotes gender stereotypes, particularly emphasizing the matrix of male aggression and female passivity. Focusing on the concept of "purity" actively denigrates victims of childhood sexual abuse and does not address the concerns of teens who were already sexually active before their sex ed began. By focusing solely on pregnancy, abstinence education also erases most queer and trans youth altogether. "Don't fuck!" isn't education; it's something someone yells at you from an open window as they drive past. Teenagers are curious about sex, and instilling teenagers with fear and shame about sex does not eradicate their curiosity. Rather, it teaches them to not vocalize their desires or their concerns, and encourages them to police and shame one another for behaviors real and perceived. This is the foundation upon which many of us build the scaffolding of our adult sex lives, expecting the ground to hold.

I was fortunate enough to get the majority of my sex education from my mother, who answered my questions outright and furnished me with several books, including her yellowing seventies edition of *Our Bodies, Ourselves*, replete with groovy illustrations of full-bush genitalia. With all my worldly wisdom, I became the sex friend, the one childhood chums pulled aside on the playground to explain blow jobs or draw a diagram of doggy style with a stick in the dirt.

By the time school sex ed rolled around, I had had nearly a decade of The Talk under my belt. My school called it Awareness of Growth, whatever the fuck that is, and the thing I remember the most is what syphilis looks like blown up big and projected on a whiteboard already crowded with facts about ancient Egypt. At least they showed us the cross-sections of genitals at all, discussed the existence of contraception in some form. So many people don't get even that. So many people learn from a sibling, a magazine that an older kid stashed in the woods behind school, or, later, from internet pornography. Learning about sex from medical illustrations and porn is like learning how to drive from a diagram of an internal combustion engine and a bunch of car commercials. One is too technical, the other sensationalized, and neither approach the substantive information you actually need.

As part of the onboarding process at the sex shop, I received twenty-five hours of sex ed, which taught me about anatomy, pleasure, different bodies and genders, and how to use every kind of sex toy in the store, as well as how to talk about it with strangers without presuming anything about their identities, experiences, or relationships. What is the internal portion of the clitoris shaped like?[*] Why do people with penises also have nipples?[†] Why does one testicle hang lower than the other?[‡] I didn't learn any of this stuff until my twenty-second year. For a couple of weeks, we met in three-hour chunks and talked about each vibrator in the store, touching them to our noses to get a sense of their real intensity. On lube day, a manager joked that she hoped I was hungry before dripping samples of twenty lubes on my hands and arms for my taste test. At the end of my training, I was handed a bag containing $700 worth of sex toys, both as a welcome gift and so that I could better describe the user experience to others. The joke I would tell on dates is that I got paid to masturbate, thinking that made me fascinating and beguiling.

Most sex shops don't look like the one I worked in, which was well lit with glass doors and windows and had everything out on display, like we sold fancy sunglasses or perfume. If you walked in, you would be greeted by between one and five cheerful young people in various flavors of queer: a willowy trans girl

---

[*] A wishbone.

[†] Because all bodies in utero develop with protogenitals resembling vulva with all the accompanying accoutrements until hormones kick in to encourage the formation of a penis and testes.

[‡] So they don't clack together like a Newton's cradle.

with blue hair and glittered eyebrows, a soft butch in denim and work boots, a chubby gay boy in a vintage tunic, all welcoming you and inviting you to look around. Plaques noting the store had received citywide awards for best customer service adorned the wall behind the registers. When I worked there, the employees chose the music, so you could shop for a cock ring while Nina Simone sang about gin.

I delighted in helping people shop for their first strap-on harness, especially the part where I showed them how to put one on and we had a little fashion show of nylon and leather underthings. I loved teaching people about the BDSM equipment, how to use everything in a way that was safe and fun and mean. And I could talk about lube ad infinitum, the various levels of viscosity, the ingredients list, the many different uses. When I presented someone with a toy that made them shriek, "Yes! Exactly!" that was job satisfaction. I pulled together a selection of toys to congratulate a woman on her divorce, and helped a guy who wanted to outfit the perfect sex dungeon. Once, I spoke to a cluster of teenage boys who came in to snicker but stayed to respectfully ask questions and buy safer sex supplies. Customers came back to shop with me over the years, so I saw my regulars through the changes in their haircuts and relationships, through different jobs and apartments.

It wasn't all sweetness. Working there was strange and occasionally dangerous. Many customers would lose all sense of themselves and of the world around them when they walked into the store. Dozens of people, for instance, asked what the sex toy was that we kept at the register, indicating a standard Swingline stapler. Several different men ambushed me with photos of their genitals on their phones, under the guise of asking for condom recommendations. I watched people spit out foil-wrapped bars of solid massage oil and had to explain to them that they were not candy—as though, if they had been, walking into a store and gumming them without purchase would have been a reasonable course of action. One man walked in during an event and asked if he could photograph my breasts, and then took offense when I told him he needed to leave the store. During my first six months working the floor, a guy said, "I want to return this," and pressed a used condom into my hand. During a Sunday shift, an inebriated woman jabbed a vibrating toy into my crotch, asking me with a slurred lilt if that's how I liked to use it. And hundreds of times over, grown adults would grab hold of a toy and swing it full force into the face of their companion.

I still don't understand how people who presumably move through the world otherwise, people who wake up and get dressed, people who conduct business and have been to a store before, could walk into an establishment, pick up merchandise they did not own, let alone understand, and hit someone in the face with it. Even from a purely pathogenic perspective, something that has been handled by the general public should not be applied to the face unless no other option is present. I would have thought that to a New Yorker, this would be like rubbing a disconcertingly buttery-to-the-touch subway pole into someone's cheek and jaw.

Soft packs were particularly prone to being used as melee weapons. Packs or packers are items shaped like a flaccid penis and testicles, to be worn in the pants to create or enhance a visible bulge. Anyone can wear them, but most of the customers who came in for them in earnest were transmasculine people. On nights and weekends, when the world was drunk, the sex educators darted around the soft packs like nervous hummingbirds. For people who did not already know what they were, a display of flaccid penises elicited laughter and revulsion. Were these the world's most disappointing dildos? Were they intended as gag gifts? Customers gravitated toward the soft packs and, as if they were brand new to Earth, picked up the packers and struck their friends or lovers. It was our job to jump in: "Hi, do you know what those are and how they are used?" (We were trained to be educational in our approach and to mask our hostility.) Most of the time, we were successful in our didactic intervention, and customers would eventually plop the packers back down and move on. Sometimes, customers waved us away with disinterest: "I don't give a fuck what they're for; they're funny as hell." Or, once we explained that they could be used by people who wanted to complete a specific kind of gender presentation, we would be met with a variation of "Oh, gross."

Sorrow from soft-pack-related violence accrued in my body. The target of the physical strike was usually unsuspecting and had not consented to be hit. I, a worker and a witness, had not consented to watch, or to allow the merchandise I sold to be used in that way. Not once in seven years had a customer asked if it was okay to use a toy as a bludgeon in my presence. Consent was something we talked about in our workshops, and I suppose people assumed consent was necessary for sex only, as if the rest of our lives passed by without our ever needing to have a single conversation about boundaries, comfort, and safety. During late-night or high-traffic shifts, and around holidays, I kept my eyes trained on the soft packs, waiting for the next strike, so I could intervene the very moment I saw contact. When we closed for the evening, those items joined the finger-fucked Fleshlights in my arms as I carried them to the employee sink and washed them in apology, working them over in my hands until the ichor ran clear. After they air dried, I dusted them with cornstarch using a fluffy makeup brush so they would be velvety to the touch and resistant to lint and grime. It was a fight against entropy, and I always lost eventually. The life of a store-display masturbation sleeve is brutal and short. Gutted displays were thrown away, which always made me wonder about the reactions of the people who rifled through our trash bags for recyclables.

Customers astonished me with the horrific comments they made. When I told shoppers about the array of skin tone color choices for dildos, many of the white people would respond to me conspiratorially, saying, "Oh come on, you know which one I want." When I did a lineup of the three variations of the same style of toy, in what the manufacturer called "vanilla," "caramel," and "chocolate" finishes, only one was the "big Black dick" to them. "They're all the same size," I would say, with a smile carved into my face, "and that kind of racialized language is not appropriate to use with me in the store. Which one would you like?" Or, once, when presented with two masturbation sleeves, one the size of a vase and the other the size of a beer can, a man looked at the smaller of the two and asked me if that was the one for Asian men. Again, I attempted a smile. "I don't know what you mean." I lied. "Can you explain your question to me?" He repeated himself, laughing. "You know! Like . . . for. Asian. Men?" "I'm sorry," I replied. "I think I'm still not getting what you're trying to ask.

Is there a way you can explain it to me to help me understand?" He sighed. "I guess what I said was inappropriate." "Yes!" I said. "It was completely inappropriate! If you have a real question that isn't racist, I'm happy to answer it." Adding insult to injury, my next customer was a well-to-do white woman with a Fendi bag. As I rang her up, she looked around the store and said, "Your job is so fun! You're so lucky! You must get to have fun all day in here!"

Although we employees were consent educators, who day after day helped strangers navigate their own boundaries, we were expected to have none ourselves. When we offered different pronouns after someone had been misgendered, or when we asked not to be touched while we talked about vibrators, the reactions from customers ranged from exaggerated overapology to nonplussed blinking to immediate white-hot rage. When my coworker and I announced that the store was closing in fifteen minutes (standard procedure that we had been trained to do gently), a white man in his thirties jabbed a finger in my face and told me that if I had been his employee, he would have fired me for being such a disrespectful bitch. His cheeks mantled when I told him that he wasn't my boss but that I'd be happy to direct him to them if he wanted to complain about me. My coworker opened the door and ordered the man and his girlfriend to leave the store. We locked up behind them, and they shook the glass door and beat the windows and screamed to be let back in.

The phone was the worst part of the job by far. A large proportion of callers were the cowards who weren't even considerate enough to harass us in person. One guy called every day for years, right around noon, to ask if we carried porn that featured

Polynesian women. One man insisted that no condom we sold would be small enough for his penis, but could I tell him about the options anyway? Many of the calls began with innocent enough questions about our merchandise, only to devolve quickly, and soon I would hear the furtive frenzy of masturbation on the other end of the line. We had been trained to simply hang up, but often after several minutes of patient and thorough customer service, hanging up was not enough to deter calls back from these guys. When I caught on to the sound of someone masturbating, I would tell them that I was going to put the phone in a bowl of batteries, which is exactly what I did: tossed the receiver into a clear glass fishbowl of C batteries and shook them like I was about to pull out a winning lotto number. The resulting sound was a loud, violent clatter, which I hoped was enough to at least delay an orgasm. We sex educators called ourselves reverse phone-sex operators, doing anything we could to kill the mood for the strangers on the other end of the line. (A decade after these incidents, I became an actual phone-sex operator; more on that later.)

One day, after playing keep away with the soft packs for hours, after asking several customers not to touch my body, after fielding racist remarks about the colors of our dildos, and after expending every last drop of kindness I had, I picked up the ringing phone to greet a caller who told me he was going to rape me. I held the phone in both fists and bellowed into it, "You can't rape me over the phone, though, can you, motherfucker?! Come on down to the store—you called the Lower East Side location. I'm here in a black dress, so you know which one I am. I will be waiting for you. Because when I see you, I'M GOING TO FUCKING MURDER YOU." With that, I slammed the receiver against the corner of the counter, as if I could snap the caller's spine on the hard laminate edge, and then hung up. I looked up into the faces of several startled customers and pasted on my customer service smile anew. "Oh, sometimes we get offensive phone calls, and I got a little angry just now. Let me know if you have any questions about anything in the store!"

On my better days, when I had gotten enough rest and had taken a day or two off from work, I could see that the deficits I saw in customer behavior were not merely individual failures of character but a structural ineptitude, an unwillingness to contend seriously with matters of the body. People made jokes or acted out because they were scared, and they were scared because they had never been appropriately acculturated to accept bodies as realities. Bodies that failed, bodies that did not live up to an abstracted ideal, bodies that made smells and tastes, bodies with parts that were small that should be big, or big that should be small, or hard when they should be soft, or soft when they should be hard. Bodies, horrifyingly, that changed, that had limits and preferences. Bodies that they could not always control. Bodies that were not enough, which is what would bring some people careering into the sex shop, looking for the missing piece that would completely satisfy themselves or their sex partners, looking for the quick fix to disguise their existential trenches. When I was really operating well, I could do what my graduate social welfare policy professor later called "lifting the lens": understanding phenomena by zooming out until I could see the tributaries that flowed into personal experience, the macro-level systems that impacted behavior. After all, how many times had I been angry at individuals for problems that were structural in nature? How many times had I fumed at people on a crowded subway car, rather than directing that energy toward the insufficient and inefficient infrastructure? How many people resent fat people on airplanes rather than the corporate greed that shrinks seats to an uncomfortable scale? (I think about this kind of thing on public transportation a lot, I guess.) Now that I am a social worker, it is that lens lifting and big picture thinking that helps me support my clients as they navigate systems that were never designed to adequately address their needs. No mental illness exists in a biologically determined vacuum. Neither are human lives determined by equally available, infinite choices that every individual has at their disposal to improve their station. Nevertheless, these beliefs form the bootstraps argument we get stuck in so often as Americans, which enables us to blame individuals for not trying hard enough to fix their circumstances, to imagine they simply have personal shortcomings that explain their situations. Of course this isn't true. An individual's experience in the world is inextricably informed by their family, the social groups they encounter, their workplace or school, their identity and the way our society understands and constructs meaning from that identity, and the systems we've created to help or harm them.* That skill, the lens lifting, started for me at the sex shop as a way to understand and interpret the bizarre and sometimes violent behavior of my customers.

---

* If you're looking for more reading on this topic specifically, the term for this theory is "social constructivism."

It was a challenge to meet customers in that place all the time. It was similarly difficult to put myself in the shoes of someone walking into the store to talk about sex toys for the very first time. I viewed the toys in the store from a place of pragmatism. My body did what my body did, and the toys did what they did. My hands could not reach the places some of my toys could reach, but I did not mistake the toys for better hands than mine. They were tools, powerless without me. Many customers, however, imbued them with the tremendous potency of demigods, viewed them with envy and suspicion, as eventual replacements, as competition, as their partners' paramour. One of my colleagues, Lena, often used the reassuring line, "Being intimidated by a sex toy in the bedroom is like a chef being intimidated by a blender!"—until one day a customer responded that her boyfriend *was* intimidated by their blender. Over the years, Lena's advice morphed into the more practical, "If you're afraid that you're going to be replaced by a piece of vibrating plastic, maybe that's a clue to think more deeply about what you bring to this relationship."

What customers came in with were symptoms of a life of learning about sex through technical diagrams, car commercials, both, or neither. What customers came in with was the fear of sexual inadequacy, which they projected onto the store. Many of them expressed that fear through violence, to themselves, to our merchandise, to their partners, to the employees, to me. Fear blunts curiosity. It forecloses on possibility. Fear teaches us not to ask. It teaches us to punish others when something happens that we don't understand. My customers had been raised on "don't fuck," which, once they started fucking, turned into "don't talk about fucking," which is easy enough to accomplish when no one provides an appropriate cultural framework for these conversations anyway. In the eyes of some of our customers, we sex educators were golems, formed from and animated by their own anxieties. Into us, they buried their pain and their anger, their shame and guilt. Surrounded by gadgets in pink and blue silicone, the sex educators I worked with absorbed, digested, translated, listened, held, demystified, soothed, and gave their own versions of The Talk, so many years late.

I loved my coworkers to the marrow of me. The people I worked alongside were strange and emotional and deeply compassionate people, mostly artists, helpers, and healers, people with radical politics. About half of my former colleagues eventually went to social work school, too; we informally referred to this practice as The Pipeline. On the surface we were retail employees, but I suspect most retail workers also wind up doubling as marriage counselors, conflict resolution practitioners, therapists, case managers, advocates. Throw in years of skill-building by talking about culturally taboo topics and you're left with someone primed for a career in helping others.

It is absurd that retail work is largely considered "unskilled" labor. Every single person I know who works in customer service, either food service or retail, works harder than any corporate flunky I've ever met. Customer service requires patience, de-escalation skills, collaboration, attention to detail while maintaining a global focus, multitasking, physical labor, and endless wellsprings of empathy and resourcefulness. What I'm trying to say is, once you can sell a pair of nipple clamps to just about any stranger in New York City, you have transferable skills.

The pay in customer service is shit because women and people of color are overrepresented in the lower rungs of the industry, and a matrix of racism and sexism erase the value of the bodies, skills, and labor of these populations. I made $12 an hour doing the kind of work that caused doctors to refer their patients to me by name. I made $12 an hour so sex therapists who made twenty times that could "pick my brain" without buying anything. Later, after a promotion, I made $16 an hour teaching workshops for medical students and was expected to perform my gratitude for my marginally improved paycheck. I developed the skills that I took into the mental health field because of the triage environment of customer service, not in spite of it.

While I don't believe in compulsory military service, I wonder what would be learned if every person in the workforce was required to at some point hold a retail or food service position. Would people treat retail employees with more respect? Would wages increase? Working retail for years sensitized me to the routine ways in which we dehumanize and disrespect other people, particularly those who hold less social clout than us. Our staff at the sex shop was a mix of queer and trans people, people with disabilities, people of color, fat people, women, sex workers, and poor people—people who already know what it feels like to be shit on and made invisible and powerless by society. Tapping into that empathy was part of what made our work so transformative, so personal. It was also what made our work exhausting, taxing, and dangerous for us. We were no less vulnerable standing in the store than we were walking around on the street.

•••

One of the strangest things about my job was walking into strangers' homes and taking over their gatherings. I would arrive at someone's doorstep for a birthday party or bachelorette, greet the group, and immediately open my luggage and start stacking sex toys in visually appealing piles; from hello to dildo in less than two minutes. My supervisor at the time forbade me from using the title I most identified with in my work (sex clown) because she thought it was derogatory and sent the wrong message to other employees. But that's what I was; I kept folks laughing while discussing the ins and outs of sex acts and sex toys, pulling bright, colorful objects out of my bag for amusement. The bachelorette parties were surreal. A door would open into an entire world, each time a different set of streamers and penis-shape decor, a different table piled high with finger food or barbecue or sushi or dinosaur-shape chicken nuggets, a different stressed out maid of honor, a different configuration of bachelorette party attendees, many of whom were strangers to one another and who spanned the spectrum from lucidity to inebriation, and somewhere prominent, me, a stranger to all, with a dildo in my mouth, trying to get through my blow job tips without a major upset. I was proud of what I did and worked hard to tailor my presentation to the mood of the room. A bachelorette group where all the participants were doctors received a different presentation from a bachelorette group of Hasidic Jewish women, who received a different presentation from a mixed-gender wedding party of queer people in their forties. That's customer service.

Nothing in my job was more exhausting than the bachelorette parties. Some participants were reluctant. Sometimes my presence was a surprise. Sometimes a bachelorette would be belligerent, screaming at me that *she* should be teaching this workshop! Sometimes the party would be so drunk that my entire presentation consisted of passing around sex toys and silently smiling while the group screeched at me. Sometimes I would sell $1,000 of merchandise and get tipped an extra $100. Sometimes I sold nothing and walked out with just my base pay (between $100 and $200). Teaching these workshops and meeting the kinds of people who were excited about wedding parties cemented for me that I never wanted to have a bachelorette party for myself. Having been on the other end of things, I knew how little magic there was in it. It all felt like work, and unfortunately it still does; my brain can't distinguish between a friend's prewedding festivity and a time for me to be on the clock.

Although the bachelorette parties would never be my favorite scene, navigating my discomfort in unfamiliar territory was a huge part of my job. In my sixth year at the sex shop, I was flown out to host a "pajama party" at a conference for young female survivors of cancer, typically breast and ovarian cancer. The conference was an opportunity for survivors to come meet one another, attend workshops, and participate in group activities. My offering was a workshop about sex and sex toys after cancer. For the rest of the weekend, I was to sit at a table in the vendor's gallery in the hotel ballroom, sell sex toys, and answer questions. I was billed as the fun part of the cancer conference.

I don't have cancer and have never had cancer. So who the fuck was I to talk to a room full of survivors about their own bodies? The week before the conference, I buried myself in research about the most common sexual issues arising after cancer or cancer treatment. Early menopause, vaginal dryness, prolapse, loss of desire. But, you know, make it fun! Writing sex education curricula involves a bit of mind reading. To write a really fantastic agenda, I have to anticipate the anxieties of this theoretical group of people who had all experienced something I had not. This one was daunting.

Then I remembered the conversations I had had with various doctors about my own sex life: the general practitioner who was convinced that I was pregnant when I, then sixteen years old and a virgin, had come to his office with the flu, or the doctor who waved away concerns about STI testing when I had done pretty much everything other than penetrative sex, or the dentist who said my mouth was so small, my boyfriend was out of luck. I remembered the medical schools in which I taught workshops and how med students sat dumbstruck while I asked them if they instructed their patients to lubricate the inside of condoms, and the even worse silence that followed when I asked if they ever inquired about their patients' satisfaction with their sex life. Did you know that most doctors are only required to take around eight hours of sex ed in medical school? I had gotten at least three times that to be allowed to sell condoms and lube. No wonder the cancer conference brought in a gal who sold vibrators for a living to do this job instead of an oncologist. Doctors and doctors-to-be struggled to talk about sex in an educational workshop about it; what were they like in their offices with sick patients, sick women?

At the conference, women shuffled past my booth, women with colorful turbans and scarves wrapped around their hairless heads, women with compression sleeves arrayed in pink zebra print, camouflage, polka dots. Women with supportive partners following closely behind them carrying the tote bags for the weekend, rubbing their backs as they wound their way through the vendor area, past displays of T-shirts emblazoned with messages like "Cancer Warrior" or "I lost my boobs and all I got was this lousy T-shirt," past pharmaceutical companies and their expensive set ups, video displays, iPads, branded pens. Cancer Incorporated, Cancer LLC, cancer as interpreted by the land of consumption. I was a sell-out, a shill.

Some of the women who saw my booth burst into tears. Others high-fived me. Still others turned heel and ran like my table was populated by a nest of hornets, and I, its bloated hive queen. Some women greeted me warmly and introduced themselves: "I'm Sharon and I have been cancer free for four years and this is my third year at the conference. Who are YOU?"

One conference-goer, a regal middle-aged lady in a drapey dress, told me she was interested in buying some lube but she had used her life savings on her cancer treatment and what pocket change she had left over went to her plane ticket to the conference. She asked for a hug and so we embraced across tasteful displays of vaginal dilators and brochures. When we separated, I realized I had left a tear stain on her outfit. She laughed.

"There's going to be a lot of that this weekend!"

Other people were ready to buy. "I haven't bought anything for myself that isn't cancer, cancer, cancer. What you got?" a younger white attendee in a tie-dyed headscarf said. I picked up a dual clitoral-vaginal vibrator and she pressed her credit card in my hand.

My upsell was lube, but lube really is perfect for everyone, especially people who have been forced into an early menopause by a hysterectomy. I handpicked the lube for the event and had selected the longest lasting and most simple hypoallergenic formulas, beautiful glass bottles of lube that looked more like perfume or luxury sunscreen and less like the industrial lavender and seafoam plastic of medical supplies. Fun! I said. Fun now that you're not lubricating the same way, I didn't say. The conference-goers looked back at me with the terror-stricken eyes I'd seen before on the faces of women reckoning with the disobedience of their own bodies. I did my best to anticipate.

"Some people feel like it's a chore to pull out a bottle of lube, and I think that happens a lot around vaginal penetration. As if you need to use this because there's something your body isn't doing but should be, you know? So I recommend using lube for all different acts and activities, like hand jobs, oral sex, masturbation, and always anal. That way it's not, like, the bad thing that has to come out for this one act or orifice. You'd be amazed how much better sex feels with lube! Seriously. I use it for absolutely everything."

Speaking without saying. We had an understanding. I added the lube to her shopping bag and swiped her card.

I spent seven hours at the table and had a one-hour break before the pajama party. I ran upstairs and put on more makeup, cried, and shoved a handful of almonds into my mouth.

I took the elevator down to the ballroom, which was an opulent affair overburdened by crystal chandeliers that hung low like branches after a storm. Around one hundred women sat in tall-backed, dark-wood chairs or shuffled around the floor in footie pajamas and fuzzy slippers. I wheeled in my bag of sex toys, arrayed my display items, greeted the crowd, and gave everyone my phone number. This was a move I used in college workshops—a way for people to ask questions anonymously, so I could give them the information they really wanted.

To my surprise, they asked questions the old-fashioned way, too. They roared with applause during a discussion of clitoral stimulation as being a necessary part of the arousal process for most people with clits. We talked about doggy style and oral sex. I did my goofy lube demo where I taste it all and pretend to be a sommelier. Attendees volunteered to Vanna White the display toys around the room while I shouted out specs. I handed the remote-control vibrator to one person and the remote to another. "Make a friend!" I said. They laughed. Oh, I felt good.

I checked my phone. These questions had a different tone.

"It makes me too sad to have my husband touch my breasts and have less sensation. How do I tell him thx."

"Single worried abt dating again w no hair. Tips on how to feel sexy??"

"Vaginal atrophy causing too much pain during sex. Anal an option and if so how and how to explain."

I took a deep breath. Time to lift the lens.

"So there are some great questions coming in over my phone so I want to make sure I have time to answer them all. I also want to say that broadly speaking, a lot of them are about how to regain confidence after the physical changes after surgery, radiation, or chemo. I want to put that into this space, that if you're feeling like you're alone in the concerns that you're having, it's very clear that you're not alone—in fact, you're in great company with other people in this very room. Different people are going to have different strategies that help them feel sexy, whether that's through dancing, or massage, or something else to help you feel pampered or adorned. And, if you're not feeling sexy right now, that's okay. Your body just did some very hard work. You put up with a lot of poking and prodding and intrusion, and you may need time to heal from that, aside from the cancer itself. So if you're not feeling super horny right now, um . . . No shit."

I stayed in the space answering questions and ringing up purchases until I was alone in the ballroom. I tossed the display sex toys back into my bag and staggered toward bed. I lay diagonal and facedown over the covers, too exhausted to care that I was likely huffing the desiccated fluids of untold guests before me.

My phone buzzed. It was Sharon from earlier that day.

"Great workshop! A bunch of the ladies are whooping it up at Fandangles. Come play!"

Fandangles was the name of the hotel's bar, but in my mind, every hotel bar is named Fandangles. I slid back into my shoes and walked over. The hallway carpet changed from muted maroon to an early nineties bowling alley pattern. I heard a shriek.

"Dildo lady!"

A tableful of women beckoned, waving me over with hands cupping wine and whiskey.

My memory stops there for the night, with exhaustion and vodka tonics acting as coconspirators. The only thing I recall is the wave of gratitude I felt to be asked along.

The following morning, my table was packed. I sold out of lube in the midafternoon and had run out of free tester packets as well. I had been thoroughly rechristened as "dildo lady," name tag be damned. I asked the sex therapist next to me to cover my table for a bathroom break, and I palmed the nearly full tester bottle of lube I had opened the day before. I spotted the regal middle-aged woman in the hotel atrium.

"Hi! I can't take this back with me on the plane," I said to her, and offered the bottle. She slipped it in her bag and winked. Speaking without saying.

The following year, I asked the store's management if I could do the event again and found out that several attendees had written in to request the same. But no, I wouldn't be returning. One of the store owners decided to go instead to save money on airfare (and just for the workshop this time, because manning the booth would be "too much work for one person"), then asked for all of my notes and research to use.

In the name of sex education, I'd taken it on the chin at this place for years. I had dealt with low pay and no health care, the repeated denials of my requests for a promotion or a raise, the lack of physical safety. This time, I felt the sting of having my work used and devalued. At the sex shop, I learned things I will never forget, not just which toys can be boiled to be disinfected and which require a damp washcloth. I learned that I was good at talking to people about sex and bodies and trauma. I learned what it felt like to care deeply for my work in an environment that used that passion against me. I stayed on for one more year, to help the retail workers unionize, and then I departed down The Pipeline for grad school.

FAQ

. . . .

In the continued spirit of education, I'd like to run you through some of the questions that burlesque performers hear over and over again. Mingling with the audience postshow can be part of the job, like actors signing autographs at the stage door, and I hope to address some of the most frequent questions with equanimity and grace so that I never have to hear them again. Here are the answers, hopefully once and for all.

What's your real name?

My love, unless you're writing me a check, there's no need for you to know. What are you, my biographer?

The name that a performer provides at the show is their name, their real name, as valid as anything on their ID or birth certificate. It's the one they are offering you, so taking it and giving it back to them with joy is the right choice. One need not dig for more. You lose the fantasy when a legal name gets involved: would you rather have a conversation with the mysterious Scarlet Sin, who just cracked whips and did a handstand, or the anodyne

Cheryl Washington,* who drives a Subaru and hasn't made it to the framer's this week like she said she would? You want the superhero, not the mild-mannered alter ego. That's as much as I prefer to give of myself, too. When I am in show mode, I only want people meeting Fancy. I don't want them to even imagine that I spent my morning seeing therapy clients and catching up on social work case notes, going to the laundromat, paying my bills. It's not relevant, it's not comfortable for me, and sometimes it's not safe to share things like that. I suspect some people want to know our names because they want to feel closer to us, but I promise, you would not feel the way that you expect if we told you. It would not be alluring. It would be banal. We'd be in proximity like two people at a bus stop, stuck together in the morass of reality, confirming once again that Santa doesn't exist and God is dead and we live in a world devoid of mystery. It's more fun if you buy into the whole story. So show your interest in us instead by collecting merch, tipping generously, and following us on social media. You'll be appreciated and adored as a fan, which is, in nearly all situations, the appropriate role and distance.

There are other reasons why a showperson is not providing you with their legal name. People who take their clothes off for strangers can be targets for creeps. I've had my fair share, like the time I advertised that night's performance by tweeting that I had hurt my finger, so my followers should attend the show to kiss it and make it better. Some guy interpreted this to mean that he should grab my hand and put my finger in his mouth while I was midconversation with someone else after the show,

---

* These are both fake names, as far as I know.

and he seemed surprised when I told him, in colorful terms, that we don't just do that to people.* Another fan figured out that I worked at the sex shop and would pop in to try to corner me into going on a date. He made his early attempts when I wasn't there, but one afternoon I saw him through the window, crossing the street toward the store. We had all been trained never to give out information about any of the employees, and to be wary of anyone who asked, so when I alerted my coworkers to his presence, they urged me to hide in the basement stockroom while they handled the situation. I heard them block his invasive questions with warm, firm protocol, followed by his petulant response as he refused to leave. When things got quieter, I crept up the first few steps of the staircase to check on the situation and saw his legs shuffling around the lube and condom display. Eventually he got bored and left, and my coworker waited until he was far gone before they gave me the all clear. I later found out he'd gotten the name of my workplace from a friend of a friend, someone without the boundaries training of a sex shop employee, someone who was probably just trying to be nice. Fans having access to a birth name can make it easier for a showperson to be found like this, and that can be a liability, especially if they're not out as a performer at their daytime workplace and with their family.

But what about the moral development of this nation's children? What would happen if you had a child and they found out about this?

---

*   "Get my finger out of your fucking mouth! What is wrong with you?"

Every once in a while you still hear of a member of the burlesque community losing their job as a teacher or day care worker
because someone went snooping into their personal life and
decided to alert the moral authorities. As if, what, a performer
would try to strip for the kids in the classroom? As if being part
of nightlife culture precludes any sense of appropriateness or
boundaries? Plenty of burlesque folks I know work as caregivers, or are parents themselves, and not a single one has a problem separating the two domains of their life, just as a bouncer
wouldn't prevent his houseguests from entering his home without first showing their ID. Americans fear sexuality so much that
we imagine that the kinds of people who express even a little
of it will get it all over everything indiscriminately, like a pen
exploding on an airplane. It's the same nonlogic as the fear of
strangers handing out Halloween candy laced with drugs. Drugs
are expensive and hard to get! Think they'd waste the good stuff
on your ugly kids? You have to pay me to dress up and take my
clothes off; I'm not doing it for free on the playground.

What's more, at the risk of sounding too, what, European?
Some children *can* understand burlesque. God, please don't let
this be the pull quote for the book. Like drunk adults, children
are drawn to sparkly things, glitter and fringe and crystals and
bedazzled feathers—and more importantly, children have bodies, and they can often have freewheeling, celebratory relationships with physical expression. The moral panic around children
and what might happen if they were exposed to certain attitudes
about nudity is ridiculous, given that young people are already
bombarded with corrosive, stigmatizing information and images

around bodies and sex from the jump. God forbid they should learn that their bodies are their own, and that bodies can be celebrated for looking a lot of different ways. God forbid they should get started on their journey toward self-expression and liberation early. When a child is born to one or more parents involved in nightlife, they grow up with these ideas as norms, and provided that their parents contextualize and apply age-appropriate boundaries around what is shown, those kids grow up to be well-adjusted and cool. Every parent will do this differently, but it might mean starting with the elements that are not sex-forward. *It's fun to dress up, and mommy plays dress up with her friends, too.* Nightlife people are present at all-ages events, like themed art modeling, drag queen story hour at libraries, or the Coney Island Mermaid Parade.* A kid might even benefit from meeting the same person in and out of costume, the cooler version of those old "Celebrities, they're just like us!" spreads from magazines. Yes, even the sparkliest people are, in fact, people. I'm not endorsing throwing the kid in the deep end at the nudie show; I'm just saying that children are more sophisticated than our society has led us to believe.

All that said, I have not relished the occasions when I have seen an underage person in the audience for one of my striptease performances. Even though I personally grew up consuming as much media as possible about fallen women, femme fatales, and bad girls in general, and even though I know that I would have

---

* An annual art parade by and for the people of New York. Look it up, or act like you know.

done anything to claw my way into a burlesque club as a tween or teen, on the other side of it, I am deeply repulsed by the experience of performing any degree of sexuality in a way that is legible to a kid. I'm also not a fan of kids at most bars, or children in adult-designated spaces as a rule. Adults have to have somewhere to go to be freaks in peace.

But again, most often it is the performer who is endangered by their work, not the real or imagined children whom they may interact with in other spheres of their lives. Many performers have a very real fear of repercussions if their families or employers were to find out about their nightlife personas. I'm not much of a kid person, but even so, my burlesque career has influenced my civilian opportunities. During my second year of graduate school in social work, an internship adviser placed me at a school working with kids, which was my last choice of setting. So I told her that there were photos of my nipples online, and I asked her if that would be a problem for her if someone at the school found out. She decided she didn't want that heat, so I settled into a clinical internship as a therapist and case manager for people working in the sex trades, and that suited me far better.

I'd love to see some righteous panic directed toward situations where people lose money, jobs, relationships, or respectability because of their proximity to the sex industry. As long as our culture continues to split off sexuality from the rest of our humanity, as long as we see women as Madonnas or whores, as long as we fear bodies and punish people who don't, burlesque performers will continue to experience risk by choosing their work—less risk than people who do porn, in-person escorting, and related forms of sex work, or club stripping, but not a negligible amount of risk, either. So I get stuck and grumpy when people follow up by asking if burlesque is a form of sex work. No, yes, sometimes, it used to be, it depends on who you ask. The real answer is that getting hung up on this categorization is less important than any initiative that materially makes life better and safer for people who sometimes work with their clothes off.

Doesn't your partner get jealous?

So the idea is that when you're dating someone, they own the exclusive rights to your sexuality? Or that sexual expression is a scarce, unrenewable resource, like the last cookie in a tin, which must be conserved at all costs for the one most deserving of consuming it? I don't know, man. What I do when I'm performing and what I do when I'm dating or in a relationship are distinctly different things. No part of my love life is improved by the presence of $600 ostrich-feather fans. No part of my stagecraft is made better by a frank conversation about how I like to be held. Of course my love life is informed by its own kind of performance of self, and my stage work is an extension of my values and preferences, but the two don't run on the same juice. I have the capacity for both, and they satisfy and delight different parts of me. Plus, I don't date the kinds of people who would get twisted up about this aspect of my life. I guess to some, the idea that other folks might experience desire when they watch me on stage is a kind of infidelity. When I hear that sort of attitude from someone, it makes me think that their idea of dating is meeting someone they like enough to trap them in a wet specimen jar in their basement. I'm no one's plastinated pig fetus. The people I click with, the ones who tend to stick around the longest, are the people who are attracted to my desire for my own freedom and, therefore, the freedom I offer them, too. The relationships that develop from that foundation are precious and expansive, and as an added bonus we get to attend shows together and throw money at my friends' asses—a cute couples activity.

For better and for worse, I've met a number of my partners through burlesque. Dipping my nib into the company ink doesn't mean my relationships are always jealousy-free, but it does make jealousy about performances and audiences, specifically, seem a bit goofy. As a rule I don't date people whom I met first as members of my fanbase. That amount of projection inevitably ends in disappointment (as above, we're at the bus stop, God is dead, etc.), and it makes my work less fun and more complicated to navigate. That said, I am not great at following this self-imposed statute, because sometimes my fans are really hot. So I will probably break it again, and soon, because I'm nothing if not an opportunist and a hypocrite.

Whatever, isn't being with someone others find desirable a cool thing, a sign of your excellent taste? Isn't it hot and nice that you're with someone that people find sexy and lovely to look at? I struggle to imagine how that is a bad thing.

Do you get hit on all the time?

Kind of? I can't tell how often I would get hit on if I weren't a burlesque performer, because even when I'm not in costume, I carry myself like a person who has received a decade's worth of applause for being naked and who talks to strangers for a living, which leads where it leads. On the other hand, I've met several people on apps who had seen me perform in the past and felt too intimidated to hit on me at the time, so the glitter doesn't always work to my advantage. Some of the smartest and sexiest performers I know have had romantic dry spells that spanned months or years because they are shy and everyone assumes that means they are unapproachable, unattainable, or out of their league. Anyway, I don't do burlesque to get dates, but I understand that people will mingle and flirt in sexually charged spaces, especially when alcohol is involved. Someone flirting with me is not inconvenient or a nuisance as long as they can recognize if I'm busy or not interested in breaking my no-fans rule that day and respond to that with speed and grace. Read the room, be open to all outcomes, and Godspeed.

Do you get horny after you perform?
No baby, *you* get horny after I perform.

Can I get a private show?
Yes, here are my rates. (When I say this, I usually never hear from that person again.)

What's your real job?
What about this work is not real? I show up when I'm hired, I do what is in my job description to do, and I make money from it, which is about as real as it gets. I don't get dental benefits or matched contributions to my 401(k), but neither do most service

industry workers. I don't make a living wage from performing alone, but neither does 44 percent of the country's labor force across industries. Working in the arts, working in nightlife, is real as hell. But when I'm asked this question, I imagine the asker wants to be comforted by hearing about a secure nine-to-five office job somewhere. This is about them, not me. They want me to assure them that nobody would rely on performance to make their living—that even artists can't actually make it as artists, so it was a good call to give up on ballet and become a landlord. I don't tell these people that I'm also a *therapist*, specifically, because that leads down a path of invasive follow-up questions or way too much personal information. So I'll usually say something like, "Oh, if you're worried that this job isn't enough for me to survive on, you can always give me some cash."

Are all burlesque performers crazy?

There's this idea that people enter the field because there is something unresolved in our lives, because we were not cared for or loved well enough, and that's why we have to perform for applause, that's why we work in the middle of the night, that's why we paint our faces with another face and tell half-truths about ourselves to strangers for not a lot of money. It's that thing that Roxie Hart says in *Chicago*: people assume that we perform "'cause none of us got enough love in our childhoods. And that's showbiz, kid."

Maybe that's true, and if it is, that's just fine. In my less charitable moments, I've called the burlesque community the "clusterfuck of Cluster B," referring to the DSM's classification for personality disorders. The presentation of histrionic personality disorder often includes being sexually provocative, overly dramatic, attention-seeking, and concerned with superficialities like physical appearance. Those symptoms are more or less the job description for a burlesque performer. Narcissistic personality disorder can include symptoms like feeling superior to others and expecting constant praise—hello, sweet applause. Meanwhile, symptoms of borderline personality disorder, a highly stigmatized diagnosis that is most often levied at women, include a fragile and shifting self-image, unstable relationships with other people, and the fear of being alone or abandoned. It wouldn't surprise me if people experiencing these feelings might gravitate toward a pursuit like burlesque for its interwoven social fabric and leeway for reinventions of the self, and as a consistent outlet for questions of self-worth and desirability.

If it's true, and we are all fucked up, so what? Look at how well we have sublimated our basest desires, our howling, hungry needs, through a more socially accepted funnel. I think the stage can be an apt container for powerful impulses, satisfying us until the next gig, which I have to imagine makes us more pleasant to be around in social settings. Build-up, climax, resolution, refractory period. It's healthy, no?

And of course, I don't think not being loved enough or having mental illness or needing praise and attention is exclusive to people working in the performing arts. Who's always mentally well? Have you actually met any of those people, and if so, would you be able to tolerate their insipid conversations, their nightmarishly even tone? I think we are all fucked in the head, that we are all okay, and that we are doing, generally speaking, the best we can do to cope.

I have to assume this question is secretly about misogyny and sex panic. Hey, is it true what they say? Are all CEOs crazy?

Do your parents know? / What do your parents think?

I get this one a lot, which is kind of a weird question to ask an adult in her thirties. I'm lucky in this respect. Yes, both of my parents know that I perform, and they knew about the sex toy store, too, even as I chose to omit other details about my life that they would have hated to know and I would have hated to tell them. When I was a little girl, they told me, in optimistic, white Boomer fashion, that I could be whatever I wanted to be, and I have taken them at their word since. I can't imagine it was easy to raise a sexually performative, provocative child. Or to tell your daughter that she can be anything—meaning, like, an architect or a teacher—and, after weighing all of the options before her, have her choose short-form nude performance art.

Throughout my childhood I dreamed about being a pole dancer, and I stayed up late enough to catch scrubbed-for-TV airings of *Showgirls*, watching Nomi Malone grinding on a greasy pole wearing digitally sketched-on underwear that stuttered with a time delay against her gyrations. The only pole in my childhood house was in our basement, a square wooden support beam. I would wrap one arm around the beam and think about a room full of eyes on me, my crotch bonking against each wooden corner as I attempted a spin. There are photos of me as a child that could tip someone off to my aspirations: one of me on a beach, maybe six years old, both hands on my hips and bending my front knee like a showgirl, my pointed foot disappearing into wet sand. A shot of me on stage from some sort of performance in the kids' section of a cruise, wearing a bikini, my cheeks and lips absurdly rouged, grinning out at the audience, arm flung in the air in celebration. After the movie adaptation of *Chicago* came out, my father caught me descending the carpeted stairs in my house at a jaunty angle like Fosse would have wanted, one step at a time, clutching my Tweety Bird bathrobe like it was the finest marabou, singing "All That Jazz." When I was ten, I trick-or-treated as Elvira, Mistress of the Dark. My parents took pictures of me in a skintight black velvet gown and black lipstick on the driveway outside my house and waved me off.

When I told my parents that I was moving to New York to do burlesque, my mother reacted as if I had told her I was running away to join the Rockettes—not with a sense of scandal, but as though becoming a burlesque performer was a far-off aspiration, something I might never achieve. A couple of years later, she came to see me perform for the first time. For her intro to this world, I chose my engagement at Kitty Nights, a long-running weekly burlesque show on Sunday nights that was $5 for five acts performed in the back room of a bar in the East Village. The audience was as full of burlesque performers as the show itself was, so it was the kind of thing you could always attend alone, knowing you'd run into someone to sit with. That night I did an act where I came out as a sexy kitty, preening and presenting myself, and in the middle of the striptease, I horked up a big fake hairball I'd made from scraps of lace onto the floor. I finished my act batting the six tassels I wore to cover all of my feline nipples. The show ended with a Jimi Hendrix number from the producer,

Fem Appeal, which blew my mom away ("She channeled his spirit!") even though now that Fem wasn't drinking anymore, she wasn't setting her guitar on fire like she used to. And when I gulped back my nerves and asked my mom if she had been scandalized by my performance, she said, "Well, come on, you've always danced like this."

My father hasn't seen me perform because it doesn't feel appropriate to him, and that makes sense to me. But he has met a bunch of my fellow performers and made me and my fellow showgirls a big smoked fish breakfast when we came through Washington, DC, on tour. He likes talking business with me, and he relishes occasions where he can act like my manager, coming up with branding opportunities for me and my future "stage engagements," to use his parlance. Despite all the reasons I may have given them to ensure the contrary, they are proud of me. I'm in the minority with that, and I'm really goddamned grateful.

That said, it's weird to ask someone who has just finished performing naked about their parents. What if they weren't okay with what I do? What if I had painfully distanced myself from them because of my work? Then you and I would be facing each other while I tell you with my tits out that I miss my father's voice. You want that experience for your night out on the town? Me neither.

How can I become a burlesque performer, too?

I am not crazy about this question. I get it. I asked the same thing after my first show. You see this once and want to be a part of it, want it to be a part of you. But most people who ask this don't want to be a professional entertainer; they want to faff around with a feather boa for an afternoon. To be clear, anyone who wants to *should* strip out of a sparkly gown, do some ass tricks, and peel a glove or two. Being glamorous and sensual feels fantastic, and it's a wonderful thing to try on. There's nothing wrong with doing that among friends, without making it a career goal, just for fun.

Some people ask this question because they're conventionally attractive, and they mistake being hot for being talented. It's a bore to watch a performer rest on that laurel for four minutes. Looks might get someone in the door, but onstage, it's worth twenty seconds, max. Often, when I'm approached by these people, they'll ask me how they can get into burlesque and then in the same breath say something fat-shamey about my body ("Where do you get the confidence?"—as if I should be living in the bowels of a Parisian opera house playing the pipe organ like the abomination I am) or something weird about their own ("Now that I got rid of my love handles, I'm finally ready!"). Being judgy about body size, thinking that being skinny is the same thing as being a compelling performer, is a way to broadcast that you do not have what it takes to make a splash on our stages. Similar but distinct are the people who think an expensive costume is enough to create stage presence. You can always tell who has thrown money at an outfit but doesn't have the chops to back it up. And, as with any type of performance, there are also folks who don't rehearse, who are uninterested in or threatened by feedback, or who just don't know how to tell a coherent story.

If you've thought through all that and you still think you've got what it takes, and you have some dance training or theater experience or costuming skills or makeup prowess, or if you're coming from a strip club or a circus or, yikes, musical theater, then okay, try taking a class at a well-respected burlesque school. Hell, go to a bunch of shows for a long time and learn as an audience member first. When you get started, work as hard as you can, show up early, remember names, and don't spread out in the dressing room.

And also . . . How do I word this next tip? You really do have to be good. Like every art form, there's some shitty burlesque out there, so unless you have something to offer your audience, think twice about whether you should charge people to see it. Burlesque is not a guaranteed way to free you from your hang-ups or your body image issues, nor will it make you a more interesting person. It isn't the surefire way to heal your trauma or undo your fucked up past. People witness the fun and think it's some kind of cure-all or roadmap. It's not. It's entertainment. It's art and labor, a cool, weird job. Some people find it cathartic (I am some people), but it's not a substitute for self-reflection and emotional processing. No one should have to pay to watch you work out your private demons unless they are receiving a show worth their money in return. You find out whether you're presenting something valuable when you work in rooms where you don't know anybody, where no one owes you attention or validation. If you can win the room over to your side, if they're following you with their eyes, if they're locked in, you're doing a good job.

The best performances I've seen share one characteristic: they are generous. So when considering what you might get out of being part of this world, imagine instead what you might have to give. And then, as you grow in your art, let the business around you be imperfect. That doesn't mean accepting any garbage it throws at you. It means allowing for the fact that where you work cannot live up to impossible standards of being a feminist body-positive utopia where no one has bad days and everything is bathed in the glow of liberation. Temper your disappointment, and this job can be both meaningful and contradictory, providing abundant gifts and breaking your heart a few times in the process. It is a miracle and a mess. If you'd rather not find that out, it's okay to just enjoy the show. Say thanks, put a tip in the bucket, and be careful about which questions you ask.

Pasties

. . . .

A pair of pasties is a miracle of engineering. To make pasties, one must fashion matching shallow cones made of fabric, foam, glue, and buckram millinery material dotted in the center with line-to-hook fishing swivels so they can be tipped with tassels and covered in glitter and rhinestones. The best pairs are symmetrical and only large enough to cover the areolae. Pasties read as a bit of magic on stage, adhered to the nipple by unknown means. Performers can jump, shake, roll around on the ground, and even pull on the tassels, and the pasties will stay on. Except when they don't. If the venue is too hot, if a performer applied lotion to their chest before getting dressed, if the adhesive is old, well. Tigger!, one of the original performers of the NYC burlesque revival (and one of the smartest hussies in town), coined the phrase "pop a pastie," which is now a popular expression of well wishes murmured among performers before taking the stage.

Venues in New York understand that pasties slip sometimes, and that audiences love it, because they're seeing something they're not supposed to. Tennessee, on the other hand, has some of the strictest blue laws in the country, and popped pasties cost performers thousands of dollars in fines. According to the so-called America at Its Best state-imposed indecency statutes, everything from the nipple down to the lower crease of the breast needs to be hidden for the duration of the performance, as well as an area on the body Johnny Law calls the "vortex," a teardrop shape that starts from the top of the butt crack and connects down to the bottom of each butt cheek. Stripteasers are therefore obliged to buy or make pretty, open-cup bras and either wear full panties or little teardrop shaped, vortex-obliterating diaper panties (imagine full briefs with the love handles chopped off of them). On top of that, performers are not allowed to touch themselves on stage in any way that could be construed as simulating sexual activity, even self-caressing. Any breast grazing must be done with the back of the hand. Try it out yourself. It's some serial killer shit. The last time I performed in Tennessee, I did an act with a friend where we portray inept, incompetent birthday strippers for hire. When I do this number in New York, I stick a pastie on so that it completely misses my nipple by an inch, which gets a slow, simmering laugh as the crowd registers the joke. For a show in Knoxville, I placed the pasties correctly and then cut out black foam half-circle slices for my underboob and taped them on with brown packaging tape so they connected with my nipple covers, obscuring any hint of flesh and transforming the shape of my breast into a mangled, droopy burrito. There's more than one way to be indecent.

I've spent more of my life thinking about how to keep nipples covered than a reality-TV censor. Making a decorated pair of pasties takes me about two hours, all told, and depending on the act, I show them on stage for maybe twenty seconds a night. This is the kind of effort-to-outcome ratio that reminds me of insects who lay dormant underground for years, breathe and eat and fuck on Earth for one day, and expire. I once met a costume designer who said to me, "A burlesque act is a whole life. You are born on stage, and you die at the end—these are givens. You are clothed, and you are naked. The minutes in between are yours to do with what you will."

Who are the gilded insects who decide to pursue a career in professional burlesque performance? Oversexed theater kids, Bettie Page obsessives, the kids who were too loose with their hips during ballet, queer people whose sexual awakenings started with David Bowie in *Labyrinth*, strippers with act concepts that won't fly at the club, assorted trollops, art loonies, fabricators, chorus line escapees, Instagram models, and (takes one to know one) sluts. We are drawn together because we are all nerds for the art form; who else would spend this much time debating the relative sparkle-to-cost ratios of Chinese crystal, resin rhinestones, DMC, or Swarovski? What size, what glue? We all have different answers, but we all know that it matters.

Burlesque performers represent a panoply of embodied human experience. There are tall performers and short ones, cis performers and trans performers, disabled performers, old performers and young performers, and performers of every race and gender. Like me, some of them are fat, and like me, some of them fall outside of the impossibly narrow limits of culturally accepted beauty. Some laymen find it clever to refer to burlesque as "stripping for ugly girls," which would be insulting if that wasn't such an exciting concept to me. Where else in life can one see all of these different kinds of bodies presented without shame, with subjectivity, eroticism, and humor? The people who attend burlesque shows with the sole intention of seeing the kind of body that reliably gives them a boner are ignoring other, more efficient ways modern technology can facilitate that experience. Those folks can stay home and jerk off until they're ready to reenter polite society.

If you are watching a show and you, personally, would not have sex with one of the performers on stage, that's fine. And it's probably mutual—we don't want to fuck you, either. If you're getting hung up on the realities of the human body in front of you (A wrinkle! A scar! A stretch mark!), then you've bought the bill of goods you've been sold by rich, eggy men in mahogany offices who hate their wives, so congratulations there. Plus, the format of burlesque shows is usually a revue, so if you don't like what you're seeing, wait five minutes and a whole new person with a different body and vibe will be on stage. If you're offended that a producer would have the audacity to book a performer who does not inspire your personal arousal, then you sound like a real treat to hang out with.

Burlesque is mostly separate from club stripping these days, although many performers do both. It is treated as a different industry with different expectations, audiences, and rates, and significantly, it is mostly perceived as a subculture or art form rather than a form of sex work. Strippers get paid by their clients/customers and pay house fees to the venue and staff to perform, whereas most burlesque performers are hired by a show's producers and paid a prearranged fee in addition to whatever cash tips they receive, which may be pooled and divided evenly. As a result, club strippers may find themselves more beholden to uphold whatever standards of beauty will net them the most money, aligning their looks with the norms of the politics of desire. Burlesque performers who conform to these standards of beauty are, by and large, more successful financially (because they are more likely to book high-profile and corporate gigs), but looking different is not as significant a barrier to entry in the industry.

Once you're in, though, you have to maintain a baseline state of obsessive madness to stick with burlesque long enough to make a living. It is an enormous amount of work that pays a pittance, especially after a string of economic recessions gutted arts funding and slowed corporate gigs to a trickle. Only major cities have enough of an industry to support full-time burlesque work, and the cost of living in those cities means it's unlikely you'll be able to make rent if your entire income comes from performing. Even if you have a way to pay your bills, you face an uphill climb in your first few years. Next to no one starts out good, and when you bomb, you bomb in the nude. The work drags you out on the town on nights and weekends and holidays when your loved ones want to see you. If you're interested in being a bad friend, a lousy partner, a liability to your day job, and a disappointment to your family, I may have a brochure for you.

But then there's the other part of it. If you're a burlesque performer, you get to design and create whatever you want, and people—a lot of people—*see* the art you make. You photosynthesize your euphoria from a spotlight in your face, and your joy unfurls like a weed under a grow light. And when you look up from your final pose of your act and your pupils shrink to adjust to the stage light, you can see that everyone in the room, the two hundred strangers who just saw you take off your clothes, people who don't owe you shit, are all standing up to applaud you because what happened on stage shook the room, made them all *feel* something—yes, even the New Yorkers. They're giving you a standing ovation because they need to physically reciprocate the energy that you alone generated and shared, and when the emcee has to pause because the cheering is drowning out their voice, and you can't tell if you're out of breath from exertion or awe, and money starts to flutter down on you like crisp autumn leaves, it is worth every second of the work.

The work. A burlesque act is a whole life. An audience will see the three to five minutes of effortless, high-energy stage time, the end product, not the hours that go into making those minutes happen. Just as with our painstakingly handcrafted pasties, we briefly flash to the audience what we have poured our time and energy into.

Prepping for a show starts the moment I wake up in the morning, because if I miscalculate the number of cups of coffee to drink, I'll be a buzzy, anxious mess, shitting every forty-five minutes, or a dead-on-arrival showgirl, too tired to sparkle. Ideally, I have slept at least seven hours, because an early evening preshow disco nap is Russian roulette; sometimes I wake up ready to dance 'til three and sometimes I wake up wrested free from time and space like a reanimated bog body.

I send my music to the DJ the night before, but sometimes I send it first thing in the morning if I'm being a little stinker. I started performing in the days when every performer brought their own music to the club, burned as a single track on a CD scrawled with a stage name and instructions or with no writing at all, depending on the level of preshow panic and chaos. Juggling these CDs for a full show of eight or ten acts was hell for the DJ, worse still when a scratched disc skipped and shuddered in the player mid-act and the performer on stage was met by a murmuration of worry rushing toward them from the audience. Some people can play with that tension, earning extra points with the crowd by acknowledging the predicament and responding with an unflappable, knowing look or playing with the silence. Others crumble into fury or fear, or shoot frantic looks up to the sound booth. The idea of that happening to me freaks me out so much that I made an act about it where I've edited fuckups into my track and have to keep adapting to the changes, à la "Duck Amuck," an old Daffy Duck cartoon. I don't miss the CD days. I like sending my MP3 in advance.

The other parts of my day happen with the volume turned down. I go to the gym and lift weights, or I have my day job or, formerly, grad school. In any given moment of mental downtime, I will think through the chessboard of nightlife logistics. What's the weather like, and what does that mean for the crowd? Ideally, it's nice out, but not so nice that most people would rather dine and drink alfresco. Rainy days sometimes deter crowds, mostly in the case of heavy thunderstorms or downpours in the hours just before the show; otherwise, people feel cooped up and often choose to go out on the town in the evening. The winter is good for show business. People are driven indoors to congregate, and burlesque and other nightlife isn't competing with summer sports or music festivals. Full moons turn the audience into animals, and it's good to plan accordingly.

Weather and holidays dictate the audience and sometimes inform what numbers I bring. But more importantly, I think about how my act fits into the greater lineup. At the Slipper Room, the owner books performers, not acts, so it's up to us what we bring. Generally speaking, if you're in the early show, don't do an act that includes full nudity, insertion, viscera, or body excretions. People will be coming straight from work, or maybe happy hour, and depending on the time of year, it might still be light out. Feather fans are an early show favorite, as are bump and grind stripteases to friendly big band songs. Newer performers might be slotted into the lineup alongside seasoned veterans of the stage. The early crowds are more timid, more sober, and less likely to heckle, so it's a friendlier way to give the new girl a shot. Usually it's a girl or a nonbinary person playing high femme.

Masculine people stripping goes over better with later audiences, drunker and less inhibited audiences, but this is a generalization. I've seen guys kill in the early set, but usually not without a jolt of nervous energy from the crowd as they realize that they're about to see a sexually presentational male body. We are so accustomed to seeing women in that light that there's comfort and familiarity in it, and a masc or gender-fucking person stripping makes people interrogate that gaze. I love that, but then again, I don't get booked often for the early show.

The earlier sets are coveted and often more lucrative. In the first of the two sets, the audience is more attentive, so if there's something that requires focus, attention, audience participation, that first set is the best bet. The lineup includes circus performers and occasionally singers or variety acts, with a selection of showgirls comprising the majority of every set. Midway through the early show, the audience is at an optimal level of inebriation— buzzed, having fun, still on their feet. They're ready to spend money; they're ready to be entertained. Production value kills in those conditions, so performers bring dazzling costumes and high-concept acts. Depending on the timing of the sets, the energy of the crowd, and the abilities of the emcee, the night can, from there, gradually escalate into orgiastic crescendo or transcendent artistry, or it can settle into surly, impatient drudgery. I've had my fair share of both.

There's a cast turnover at midnight, and things evolve or devolve from there. The midnight show promises to be looser and more debauched. Performers often bring their wild, weird numbers. Performers deep-throat dildos; tie themselves into *shibari*; strip out of matted, well-worn fur costumes of trademark characters. Are you smoking a joint on stage while you sit nude behind placards bearing the words to Bob Dylan's "Subterranean Homesick Blues"?* Are you inserting a remote-control vibrator and handing the controller to the crowd?† Are you dangling from a trapeze in nothing but red patent boots and a butt plug?‡ Welcome to the midnight set! Most of the audience is well toasted by the late show. Vodka sodas fall out of the hands of clumsy bachelorettes in the balcony and baptize couples in their floor seats. The octogenarian circus legend sitting at a reserved cabaret table up front with a glass bottle of milk—one that he drinks over the course of the night and fills with urine when he's done—is asleep in his chair. Detritus builds up on the floor of the bar like sawdust in a woodworking shop, napkins and confetti, glitter, straws, candle wax, lost earrings, errant rhinestones that popped off during a particularly energetic glove peel. Inevitably, some guy, somewhere, is yelling.

No matter the show, if the lineup is populated by folks who do one kind of act, it's a good idea to bring something else. If I'm with Kewpie doll rockabilly gals who pop into drop splits like marionettes, I'll bring something with narrative, or something funny. If folks in the lineup are skilled at the classic bump and grind striptease, I don't want to offer an act of mine that approximates the same but with less expertise. Contrast sets one up for

---

*   Hi, Stormy Leather.

†   Hey, Jenny C'est Quoi.

‡   Someone should steal this concept.

success, and it creates a more varied viewing experience for the audience. Despite our best efforts, we fuck this up sometimes, and some nights I find myself backstage with three other girls in red gowns and boas, shrugging and making the most of it. We all get naked in the end. (For the record, I've never gotten complaints that there were too many red dresses.)

At the Slipper Room, every performer brings two numbers. I messed that up big time during my audition performance at the venue years ago when I only brought one. Explaining my mistake to the host and DJ was mortifying, and I worked the curtain for every performer after me as penance, wanting to earn my keep. Now I know better. Which act to do first and which to do second is an important decision. If I'm bringing an act that involves mess, liquid, or something that might muss up my makeup, I want to do that second. If I get fully naked in one of my numbers, also second. If I'm debuting a new act, I can choose: would I rather get the stress of a new routine out of the way, or would I rather win over the audience first before possibly bombing? If the act is sad, if it's serious, would I rather have that be how folks meet me or how they leave me?

Did I mention that the performers also go-go dance? The two full rotations in the show are bookended by interstitial breaks, twentyish minutes for the audience to order more drinks, to chat, to fuck in the bathroom, to go out and smoke. They can tip one of the performers, who has changed into something strappy to dance on stage in front of the curtain, while another performer does a lap around the room with a champagne bucket, collecting cash from the shy spectators. Given that I'm probably going to be asking for more money at the halfway mark of the show, and given that people will give me more money if they like me, I always consider what acts will accomplish that perfect facsimile of a relationship.

These are the things I think about while I am chewing my cud and dissociating at my desk or on the subway. Lunch, by the way, is also an important calculation. No Chipotle on show day. You know why.

When I get home from work, I pack my suitcase. Each act, on the modest end, requires a pair of heels; pasties; panties; a bra; a pair of gloves; legwear, like stockings; a shimmy belt; a gown; a wig; and a hair accessory, like a sparkly flower or an ostrich-feather headdress. Or maybe, depending on the act, a diaper, a bag of "cocaine" (usually flour or baby powder, neither of which is fun to snort, but doing a line of baking soda *sucks*, trust me), a rhine-stoned rattle, a wig, a bonnet, a Tupperware container of fake poop according to your proprietary recipe (everyone has their own, depending on the desired effect), a towel, and baby wipes. Or your multipiece crab carapace, an inflatable lemon wedge, and underthings with bejeweled crabs hanging off an exaggerated pubic merkin. For example. But remember, two acts, so do this inventory process for each number. Every fussy piece that is flung off in the course of the striptease is essential for the choreography. When I pack, I listen to my track and act out the number a few times, to make sure I have every single item accounted for. If the costume is going to get wet during the act, I bring a plastic bag to carry it home in. Don't forget at the end of the night to remove the garment from the bag and hang it to dry. No one likes microbes.

Then I pack the other, more invisible necessities of burlesque. First, pastie tape, the adhesive I use to stick my nipple tassels onto my body. The tape works anywhere you need something to adhere to the body temporarily and can be used in a pinch if your heel falls off your shoe and you just need to get through the next five minutes on stage intact (the shoe, and you). I pretape my pasties to save a minute during quick changes, so all I need to do is peel off the back of the tape and adhere. It's stripper mise en place. I tend to carry my pasties in metal boxes, often repurposed after I finish my loose-leaf tea. A rigid container keeps them from getting smashed down and deformed in transit. If I can, I always bring extra tape. Every single one of us art strippers has at one time been the person who forgot their tape, and every single one of us has at one time been the person who could lend some and bail out a colleague in need. When I buy pastie tape, I think of half the roll as a tithe, to be given away to others. In return I use my fair share of others' tape without guilt. (Save the waxy tape backings for postshow, by the way. They're great for scraping off glitter lipstick without wiping the stuff all over your face. It's an old drag queen tip, and old drag queens know everything.)

Makeup wipes are preferable to a bottle of remover, which knows exactly how to tactically explode on a dry-clean-only peignoir ten minutes before showtime. It's not worth the risk. If the act is messy, a towel and baby wipes are essentials. You don't want to be the person wiping fake vomit off your nude body with flimsy, Soviet-style toilet paper in a drafty foyer. Most venues don't have showers, but a couple do, in which case, it's nice to bring flip-flops so that you can shower without risking a festive case of athlete's foot.

I always carry a small pair of scissors in my bag, along with a lighter and a book of matches, a mini sewing kit, and safety pins. Every possible bad thing that could happen to a garment or prop has happened. People forget their lighter for their smoke fetish act, for their flaming torch, for their drippy candle, and I can unfuck their entire night by pulling out a fire starter. Straps pop off and pins put them back on serviceably enough. Buttons fly, especially when your job is to rip off your clothes with élan, and if there's enough time before or after the show, they can be sewn back on before it's a liability for the number. I've made yearslong friendships because I offered one of these items in a time of need, struck up a conversation with one of my heroes and idols as they whip-stitched their thong back together. Some compassionate producers have a basket with these items and things like granola bars, bottled water, and Band-Aids. The producers who supply those comfort items tend to be strippers themselves. It's an expression of empathy.

I can't forget a go-go outfit. Because I'm going to be dancing for fifteen minutes straight during my go-go set, I tend to pack a more orthopedic pair of shoes. I make more money when I'm wearing high heels, but I also make more money when I'm able to dance freely and throw myself around. I have endless admiration for the strippers of the world who can manage both at the same time, who look light on their feet in eight-inch Pleasers. It's not me, and I know to play to my strengths. Sometimes, I'll go-go in character, so maybe I'll be a lumberjack in a bra, a flannel shirt, and hiking boots, or a mermaid in scaly booty shorts and a bra that suggests mermaid shells. Whatever I wear, I like it to be strappy, which helps give people more options as to where and how to tip me. Those garments do a better job at holding the cash against my body than something like a baby-doll nightie. I also make sure to have a couple of $1 bills packed with my go-go outfit. Before I hit the go-go box, I pretip myself, tucking a buck into a visible strap to cue the audience that they are supposed to present me with their cash. No matter how many times I say otherwise, some people believe it's rude to give me money. I promise, handing people strings-free cash is the best etiquette in the world, and is considered particularly polite in nightlife culture. They don't teach you that at finishing school, maybe, but tucking money into my bra straps is what my bra is there for.

You would be amazed at what people think they "get" for their money, however. I'm a fan of disinterested generosity. If you like my show and you appreciate what I'm doing, that's worth a tip. You don't get anything extra for a $1 bill. Try tipping in twenties and you might have better luck.

I will also pack a mirror. Having my own reflective surface expands my options about where I can finish my look, removes me from any competition for the spots in front of the dressing room mirrors, and also allows me to capture any angle of decent light. People think that back stages are glamorous. Not in New York, they're not. They more closely resemble the makeshift oubliettes of Eastern European kidnapping victims. If you end up in a backstage area for a burlesque show that features performers from all over the world, you can always tell the New Yorkers, because they have their own mirrors and lights, and everything they brought packs down into a single suitcase or shoulder bag. After all, we're taking the train home.

Once my bag is zipped and ready to go, I take a shower and begin the multiphasic hair removal process; that is, I take great pains to render myself as smooth and slick as a dolphin darting through the surf. For a dark-haired Jewess with a hormone imbalance, the vicious speed of hair growth on my body is not unlike that of a Play Doh pasta extruder. In a Sisyphean thrash against entropy, I remove my leg hair, front and back, all the way up, and eradicate my pit hair. Depending on the act I'm doing, I'll shave or trim my bush, too. I'll also remove the hair on my ass depending on my costume that night and the venue's lighting setup. A photographer friend of mine once told me about sitting in the front row for a show where a performer bent over in a thong in red lighting (a color that inhibits the eye's ability to distinguish between darker shades, so everything just shows up black), and he was convinced she had shit herself until he looked back at the photos and discovered it had been a thicket of ass hair. The story makes me want to pass away in vicarious embarrassment, so I squat over a mirror and take my time. I leave my arm hair, even though I have more of it than I like. If I remove it, it doesn't grow back right. So fuck it, punk rock.

I wish I could do my job without wearing makeup, but I become a different person when I am wearing a full face, and that's the person people pay to see. That's the inscrutable work of being femme, anyway: the seamless orchestration and application of the contents of two dozen tiny bottles of goo that cost thirty bucks each. My mother didn't teach me this stuff, because she doesn't wear makeup herself, beyond a little kohl on the corners of her eyes. I learned how to paint my face through trial and error, and error, and unforgivable error, refining my techniques by asking the other girls backstage and observing what they did to perfect their looks. Fortunately, there is no expectation that the makeup look for burlesque will appear natural. So if it's clear that I did not wake up with overdrawn glitter lips, mink eyelashes, and a swooshy cat eye, that's fine. I don't have to pretend that I didn't try, which is healing, in a way. The work of womanhood is all over my face.

The process of going from a bare face to a full beat can take as little time as twenty minutes for a basic showgirl look, or it can stretch into twice or three times that for a specialty look. If it's raining or humid or I know the venue has a well-lit dressing room, I'll save lips and lashes for the backstage vanity mirror. Otherwise, I'll pat red ecofriendly cosmetic glitter into my still-drying liquid lipstick, adding a touch of gold glitter in the center of my bottom lip for a wet, full, scintillating look. If I'm on a stalled subway car and I'm going to be late, I will do my makeup on the train. I despise it but it's a showgirl rite of passage. New performers freak out about deviating from their perfect plan. Seasoned performers assume endemic chaos and are not rattled by such things. I've done my look with no mirror or light in the room except for my phone. If it sounds like I'm bragging, I am.

When I'm done with as much face as I'm doing at home, I fill up my water bottle, tuck it into my suitcase, get my purse, and call a cab or hop on the subway. It's not glamorous, bumping up and down the subway stairs with a suitcase or sweating on a summer platform, my face melting in the morgue-like lighting. But it's cheap, and spending $2.75 to get to, say, Coney Island beats a $45 cab ride that might take just as long. The Slipper Room is just over a bridge for me, so I indulge my inner Little Lord Fauntleroy with a $12 taxi.

Are you tired yet? When I pull up to the venue, the show starts in an hour. On a Friday or Saturday night, Manhattan's Lower East Side teems with lumbering bros, women teetering in heels they are not sober enough to manage, and hordes of anyone longing to puke in the gutter. The neighborhood always emanates that soused, vile 3-a.m.-on-New-Year's-Day vibe. I consider it a success if I can travel from car to stage door in ten seconds or less, barely touching the sidewalk, like a water insect skimming across a stagnant pond. It's the fall of Rome every weekend on the LES. It's pizza crusts, used condoms, cigarette butts, and firework-shape sprays of vomit. It's apocalyptic.

The Slipper Room is tucked away on the second floor of a building on the corner of Drunk Couple Fucks on Car Street and NYU Bro Fistfight Avenue—you know that intersection, right? Inside, up the staircase, everything is warm, decked out in burgundy and gold and chocolatey wood, the inside of a music box, with all the walls covered in brocade blackout curtains or ornate velvety wallpaper. I greet the door person, the bartenders, the producer, the host, and drag my suitcase backstage.

Backstage. The burlesque bus terminal. The holding cell. The public private space. Performers shift and pace like big cats stalking back and forth, waiting for the gates to go down, knowing they will soon be face to face with the meat. A showgirl throws a long, stockinged leg over a chair and texts while she stretches. One girl brings her dog, who mostly sleeps in her suitcase but who has walked across the stage during an act at least once. We greet with air kisses. No one wants to mess up anyone else's applied face.

During the show, backstage is the refuge. A performer with a high fever who couldn't find a replacement executes an athletic striptease and then runs backstage once the curtain has closed to stick their head in the toilet—quietly, so the audience can't hear. The aerialist counts out the piles of tip money. The vogue dancer takes selfies when she should be taking her turn working the pulley for the curtain for the other acts. The new girl downs a glass of champagne.

At the Slip, backstage is its own designated space, but at some places, the cast is shoved into a walk-in closet or, honest to God, a refrigerated meat locker partially occupied by aging sides of beef. At any given time, there are between three and twelve other people in there with me, dressing, undressing, brushing hair out from rollers, steaming garments. If the host for the early set is running long with bloviating anecdotes, all of this will actually be happening in an adjoining hallway, because the previous cast is still backstage. A cocktail waitress will pop in and take orders; mine is usually a seltzer with lime. Some girls like or need a drink before the show, but I can't stand the idea of being even a little drunk on stage to start. In the dark, waiting for my drink, standing over my open suitcase, I'll finish my makeup look, put on my wig, unpeel and stick on my pasties, and put on the rest of my costume. At some point in that process, I'll do a little stretching and shimmy my shoulders to make sure my tassels aren't caught in my wig or tucked under my breasts. If I'm later in the show order, I have more time to hang out and chill. If I'm hosting the show, everything needs to be set right away because I'm going on first. Just writing about this makes my stomach flip.

I get squirrelly and quiet before a show. Most other folks are chatty, gossipy, or otherwise socially extroverted backstage. If I'm doing a newer act or one I haven't performed in a long time, I'll duck out into the hallway, listen to it on headphones, and mime through the act one last time. At the Slipper Room, the host, DJ, and performers hash out the lineup together during the half hour before showtime. If I am hosting the show, this is when I'll start to feel queasy. I thought the nausea would go away once I had a few years of performing experience under my rhinestone belt, but the feeling persists. The DJ writes out the set list in Sharpie and sticks it onto a clipboard backstage, next to the dimmer switch, which is lowered from makeup-application bright to restaurant ambiance for the duration of the show to prevent light leaks that might distract from the stage.

I stand backstage as the DJ makes the announcement for people to grab their seats, and I hear the audience shuffling, cheering, and chatting, settling in for showtime. The thick red velvet curtains separating me from them are a uterine membrane. My stomach makes its own prenatal contractions as the fog machines shudder on, filling the stage area with fragrant, atmospheric smoke. The multicolored gobo lights click on, cutting through the fog with a purple glare. I make sure the mic is on, its batteries full, and adjust the mic stand so it is at my height. The DJ plays the last track on the preshow list; if I'm ever in a coffee shop or grocery store and that song plays over its speakers, I have to leave and come back, because the Pavlovian adrenaline rush is too intense.

Behind the curtain, shifting my weight in my heels, I begin to regret my life choices. I wish I were at home with my cat. I wish I were in bed, asleep. I wish I hadn't chosen a path that forces me to shred my nerves, stay up late, live a double life. I regret that I do something that takes so much time and precision, so much energy, that makes so little money. I hate the audience, but most of all I hate myself. I hate everything that has led me to this cursed stage. I hate my body. I hate my costume. I hate my makeup. I hate, I hate, and a big bubble of vomit rises in my throat as the DJ says my name. I swallow it back. A cast member cached away in the corner of the stage pulls the rope that opens the curtain. Before me, the only thing I can see is a growing expanse of white light. After labor, I am born on stage. I am in my minutes. I am weightless and sublime. I know exactly what to do. *Pop a pastie, bitch.*

Doing Yourself

. . . .

I came off the line of creation with factory defects. I have
PCOS, or polycystic ovarian syndrome, which means that my
ovaries are riddled with pearl-like cysts that mess with my hormones. More specifically, they contribute to an excess of andro-
gens, or masculinizing sex hormones, in my body, which can
prevent, delay, or complicate ovulation and menstruation. The
condition is correlated with excess body hair growth, male pattern baldness, and infertility, and is one of the main contributing
factors for why I am fat. This is not a rare condition; something
like 10 percent of people with ovaries also have PCOS. We don't
really know what causes it and we don't have "treatments," per
se. It's one of those conditions that gets *managed*, like my ovaries are insubordinate employees. I think of my menstruation
as something liminal and unreliable, something that starts and
ends at odd intervals and that, over the course of my life, I will
come to pass through altogether, moving through that phase of
life less like sand through an hourglass and more like the weird
jog people do after they trip. I was taught to tick off my period

in twenty-eight-day cycles on my middle school planner, which never fit my body's tempo. Then it disappeared for eleven months without warning when I was in high school. When it returned, it poured from me in flash floods. I became accustomed to the marine salinity of clotted blood, which pooled between my legs, handfuls of the stuff. I made peace with my existence as a performance of self-contained body horror. This breach of womanhood, the stop-start, was another thing my adolescent body did not know how to do well.

I was diagnosed with PCOS in my senior year of high school, not by a doctor but by the fat and cheerful laser hair removal practitioner with whom I spent countless hours in a futile collaborative attempt to obliterate the dark leg hair from my upper thighs. "You can ask your doctor to do a test for it if you don't believe me," she said, "but there's no point in wasting your money. It's what you have." I found a kind of comfort with her in that office, or as much as could be expected with someone wielding a laser gun. Her no-nonsense attitude was worth the price of admission: engaging with the office's front-desk person, who, without looking at my chart, scanned my face and said, "You're here for your mustache, right?"

My gynecologist subsequently confirmed the electrologist's diagnosis. My family sobbed on the couch; my parents from grief and I from relief. I told my parents that I never wanted to hear their input about my diet or my body ever again, and that I would remove myself from any such conversations that arose. Until then, it had been assumed by most parties that my weight gain during puberty was due to a penchant for soda or something—to the point where an endocrinologist was convinced I was lying to her about my Coke habit. This was proof that I was fat for reasons other than my sloth or my indulgence. Diagnosis was my moral vindication.

It took me decades to realize that, because of my PCOS symptoms, I was experiencing dysphoria. No one helped me name the ice-water feeling in my stomach as I watched my face's reflection crowd with ever-darkening curls of facial hair. I was going through the wrong kind of puberty. A doctor prescribed me spironolactone, a big, stinking hormonal supplement that can decrease body hair growth—it's most often prescribed to trans women and to PCOS "cysters" (a word I hate more than hell itself), two groups of women who might be seeking a different hormonal balance than the chef's choice for their gender presentation. I took the pills well into college, and their diuretic quality led my mother to encourage me to piss in a cooking pot in my dorm room during the night so that I wouldn't have to walk down the hall every couple of hours. (I was living in an open double room with a wonderful roommate who put up with a lot, but I don't think she would have stuck around if she had caught me surreptitiously whizzing in our mac and cheese pot, staring at her from the darkness.) I've been on a number of different kinds of birth control, taken vitamins, eaten a lot of cinnamon, a lot of dark leafy greens, a lot of green tea. I've worked out a lot. I've avoided alcohol. I've done everything short of going on metformin, a drug that is shown to have some salutary effects on people with PCOS but involves enduring an adjustment period of several months of nonstop gas and diarrhea. Who's got that kind of time? I can't imagine a more complete definition of a luxurious schedule than having six months to set aside to literally fart around.

In the midst of understanding that my body was going to torment me with a series of Judas-worthy betrayals, I started having sex. My first time was with my first boyfriend, a singer-songwriter in his early thirties. I was in love with him, which was not enough to keep me from realizing that the sex was bad, and that the badness wasn't my fault. He dumped me a week later in the spring of my freshman year of college, citing the pressure of being my first, and he immediately started up with a seventeen-year-old from Myspace. For me, heartbreak meant spending two months throwing up from shock and grief. People congratulated me on my weight loss. Meanwhile, I was puking between cars, in my lap in class, in the multistall gender-neutral bathrooms of my freshman dorm. That was the secret, so try selling that on late-night TV. Vomit long and hard over a man in his thirties who fucks teens and writes Starbucks-playlist music, and watch the pounds melt away.

My next mission was to have sex again, so that my nonvirginity couldn't be attributed to just that one disappointment. Quickly, I learned that for men who are ashamed of fucking a fat woman, first base is a text, second base is going straight to his place when he's sure no one else is around, and third base is whatever he's been meaning to do to someone since seeing it on a tube site, whatever combination of keywords stir his lust and curiosity. BBW, something something. BBW + doggy-style cumshot. BBW + sloppy blow job. BBW, big beautiful woman, the euphemism that gazes in from outside at bodies like mine as they lay passive and receptive, spread and waxed, skin shiny in bad lighting. Fourth base is whatever happens after he comes, whether he offers me a paper towel, spreads his seed on my skin with a clumsy finger like margarine on toast, or ties off the condom and tosses it on my floor. Fifth base is going outside. There is no fifth base—these men would never be seen with me outside, in the daylight, with their friends.

When the person fucking me was ashamed of me, it coiled out of their mouth like steam. It echoed in their rough, uncareful touch, which yanked at me as if I were carrot greens; it was in the wild, roving gaze that inventoried everything but my eyes. But the sex was urgent. It contained need and vigor and contempt, which was its own kind of vitality. When someone is ashamed of you, you'll be fucked thoroughly but not well.

It used to be novel to me that someone might desire my body, my collection of private horrors, and I veered into the stereotype of the grateful, oversexed fat girl like a fly frying on a bulb. I became a girl who worked harder at being charming and sexy and fucked better because she had to. I could, I thought, compensate for my shortcomings with my willingness and my enthusiasm. I could, I thought, take all the hatred into myself and distill a line of poetry from it, a defiant act of fat girl alchemy. I would have rather set myself on fire than become pitied, than become the girl who wore a T-shirt in the pool. So I showed off the round body that was mine but not mine, the one PCOS puberty had tacked onto me, displaying myself as an attempt to run in the opposite direction of my disgust. There just weren't any other options that appealed to me. Being slutty was the only way of finding a shred of agency.

Meanwhile, I learned to hold my tongue when dudes wanted to fuck me and not date me. The tacit knowledge of being someone else's cupboard skeleton sat between my lips and my front teeth, held in my mouth like decaying chewing gum. There's a tightness to containing the secret, to being someone's shame, smiling the stretched, thin smile of someone who has learned that she must settle if she is going to be touched. When my phone buzzed after midnight and I opened it to greet a text asking me to come over, I held in the sound of my disappointment, which if rendered audible would place the punctuation on the end of that loud, unspoken sentence: *I am ashamed of being seen with you.* I walked away from encounters with the feeling of being off-loaded like a corpse from the bed of a pickup truck. I'd take his shame and rot with it. I used my mouth for something else, to prove my worth, skill, value. I got so good with my mouth that I could hold my tongue—and his, too.

I know how to make people come. As a phone sex operator, I listen for the rising tension in a man's voice, his ragged breathing, before I deploy a barrage of his favorite keywords to finish to. When I help out a cam-girl friend, logging on for sessions with paying men in luchador masks or makeshift ball gags, I know exactly how to feign enthusiasm. As a sex educator, I equipped groups of forty-five women in my free twenty-minute workshops with ten brand-new ways to touch their clits when they got home. And my superpower follows me when I meet up with men, like when an ER doctor I was rebounding with hounded me over text for weeks to know what exactly I did with my mouth so he could ask for it with the next girl; or with my part-time sugar daddy who, after our hookups, sometimes needed to collect himself in the other room before he could speak again; or with the divorced cuckold I played around with who said having sex with me was like playing basketball with LeBron James. "How are you always thinking ten steps ahead of me?" he asked me once, red-faced, from his knees.

I'm not a mind reader. *Neither are any of you!* I would remind customers. After my workshops, a woman might raise a hand and ask me if I am good at sex.

"Yes."

The crowd would shift in their fold-out chairs and giggle. I'd wait a beat, to let the idea hang, to let them hear that I didn't bat away my competence, to let them imagine what sex with me must be like.

"But not because I can unhinge my jaw or fold into a pretzel! I don't have secret superpowers. I'm good at sex because I know how to communicate, and I'm not afraid of talking to my partners about what I need and what my boundaries are."

A compelling lie at first, but mostly, now, it's true. I talked to the divorced cuckold. We negotiated beforehand and on the fly. I wasn't a mind reader. But I could read his body. I knew what it meant when his jaw tensed, when he paused before responding, when he held his breath. There's no magic trick to it, but that's what it can feel like when someone is paying attention to you that deeply. When I talked about sex with people at the sex shop, I wanted to make them feel like what they wanted was fun and fine, and that they could have it if they wanted. I could sell someone a new vibrator in a way that made them feel—let me wheeze out this word—*empowered*. I could tell them the difference between twenty water-based lubricants and how they feel to jack off with, while gesturing at bottles arrayed on a friendly little shelf like a real estate agent staging a lovely breakfast nook. I could tell the story implicit in all retail: *buy this and you won't be sad*. I didn't have the heart to tell them that some days they will still fuck themselves in the bloodless morning like I do, wracked with lamentation for the bigness of their bed, its softness and theirs, their skin that only they are touching. I didn't have the heart to tell them that whatever they bought from me wouldn't fix anything that someone else had broken inside them.

We all touch ourselves in different ways. I could tell customers that, with my sex educator hat on, and it could mean that although there are some common themes around erogenous zones and patterns of stimulation, no one person likes to be fucked the exact same way as someone else. So for people learning how to masturbate, mimicking precisely the way I'd suggest you use a toy is less important than being completely checked in with yourself, noting the different sensations you feel as you experiment. What I like and what you turn out to like may not be the same at all, which is great, actually—not a departure point for anxiety but a reminder of a human truth, of our little fingerprints of difference.

We all touch ourselves in different ways, and sometimes those ways can be a form of storytelling. We curl our spines around our fantasies, leaning in as to a campfire in the cold. We tell ourselves stories about ourselves, tall tales that enliven us and torture us and turn us on. And when we masturbate, we root between our legs, playing with the ghosts we have made, even when we know we will be left haunted by the fears that we've sexualized, the wishes we cannot fulfill. We fling ourselves off the cliffs of desire, die the little death, and do not die.

I don't always like my stories. It is perhaps no surprise, then, that it's easier for me to become someone else's fantasy than to have fantasies of my own. Mine hurt. If I ever fulfill one, it moves from the gossamer realm of fantasy to reality and becomes dull and silly. Meanwhile, my unfulfilled wishes fester and bloom inside of me, nibble away at my viscera, and crowd out any sense of satisfaction. So if I can satisfy someone else's narrative and experience their full pleasure through them instead, why wouldn't I do that? It's cleaner to try to disappear into the imagination of the other. It's less fraught than dealing with my own humanity.

I was fed this story early, when I was a baby being socialized into but not yet failing at womanhood: that the only women worthy of love were women who could contort themselves into closed ecosystems, who could be completely self-sustaining. These were women who could suck the exhaust out of their own pipes and convert it into clean air to breathe, women with an endless capacity to hold and support their men, women who didn't like books unless they were the books their boyfriends liked, women without opinions about art, women without opinions about sex, women who only wrote things that were nonthreatening. To be loved I would have to be malleable. To be loved I would have to be nothing at all, until a man thought to come by and create me, to breathe life into my clay. And to be that kind of woman, the right kind of woman, I'd have to be hairless, thin, and frail, like a cat fetus. I learned that from everywhere. I learned that from sitting in the soup we're all boiling to bits in. I learned that from seeing myself represented nowhere, seeing no one with my body type being happy, loved, accepted, desired. I learned that through the shame that passed into my mouth, mixed with men's spit and semen.

But this is all preamble to what I would rather say about my body, its pieces and its whole. Loving my body has been a struggle for a long time, since long before burlesque, before I was sexually active, before I had words for gender identity or the experience of gender dysphoria. I just knew that I felt "off," not the way a woman should, not soft enough in some places and too hopelessly soft in others. I hated my belly; I still have a hard time with it, despite loving the bellies of others with my whole self. I feel like I'm slogging upriver sometimes, the current of my body and hormones telling me how unfeminine and unwomanly, how somewhat in between I am. An androgenic cocktail, the Charybdis that pulls me closer to the center when I am so much more interested in being on one shore. I'm comfortable in femme, in hard femme, the spiked and gold-plated femininity of my everyday presentation. But this daily effort takes hours of work and illusion and it *slips*. It falls apart too easily. Bleach and razors and corsets and makeup and wigs and drugs—I am not always what I say I am. Proof of my womanhood lies in the work itself, "woman" representing not so much an identity as a set of actions, an expenditure of labor. Haven't you heard people whispering in scorn about how a woman has "let herself go"? What is hidden in those words? The fear of someone who has given herself permission to set off in the direction she actually prefers? Am I, then, some sort of Frankenstein's monster, a creation cobbled together from my childhood dreams and fears? Full burlesque drag covers the surgical seams and spackles over the inconsistencies. But I do not feel like a monster, nor a sideshow at a carnival, a bearded lady, a fat body to be gawked at. I am a configuration of bone and blood and skin, firm flesh and soft pillowy fat, and when I invite someone into my body, it's like welcoming a guest into my home. I want to offer comfort and be comforted by the company.

I am not at war with the body I wake up in. We've slowly built up an armistice, even though there are and may always be moments that threaten to rupture the detente. There is no skinny woman inside of me waiting to get out, to be unshackled from cuffs of fat. If there ever was, I have interred her, Cask of Amontillado–style, and left her for dust. There is an effervescence in the unruliness of my body. Feeling fat and ugly has gone from feeling like a tremendous burden to feeling like some kind of inverted superpower. I have learned, as a function of my continued existence and the abject joy I experience, that being beautiful is not the most important thing in the world, and so being ugly is not the worst thing I can be. The best phrase our wretched, commodified vocabulary can come up with to describe this is "body positive," which I'm not. I stopped believing in those words when an ad parroted them back to me so that I might buy

$40 soap. I realized the phrase had been offered in my life as a consolation prize, an individual balm for living in a society that hates fat people. I do not owe the world positivity when it seeks to punish and destroy people who look like I do; the onus is not on me to be relentlessly cheerful about this journey. Moving toward pleasure is only useful if it also moves us toward liberation. Which is why I sometimes say, when I'm feeling contrarian, that no one should have a body. I'll wave my Jewish hands over this sentiment and say a combination of prayer and curse: may we all become a fine, damp mist. The only beings who have it right when it comes to bodies are caterpillars. A caterpillar does not go into its chrysalis and move its body around until it becomes a butterfly. Rather, it dissolves all of its own tissues by releasing the enzymes it needs to digest itself, to unmake itself completely. That's self-actualization, baby. Good for them.

I'm not a caterpillar, of course. I have a human body, one that has known and craves the sensation of soft, nurturing touch. Not everyone I slept with when I was younger was ashamed of their desire for me. I tend to those memories and those men with the fretting care of a gardener watching seeds germinate in wet napkins. I gather their loving kindness. When I was nineteen, a man I was sleeping with off and on knocked on the bathroom door to let himself into the shower with me, and with hands soft with curiosity, devoid of grasping need, he worked shampoo into my scalp in loose, careful circles. His face neutral, his jaw relaxed, he watched me for any tang of discomfort, which did not come. He swiped rivulets of lather off my forehead with his thumb, keeping my eyes clear and open. His touch transfixed me. I gazed up at him, and he gazed down at me, not with love but with care, like I was a passage worthy of a close reading. I sewed the memory into me, a patch over a threadbare place. The color has faded but the stitches have held.

Another quilted piece, the invitation to a new love's apartment, where he and his spouse and the spouse's boyfriend were making dinner for the anniversary of their marriage. Hurricane Sandy had snuffed out the subway, and gray floodwaters were still gurgling on the road. I hailed the improbable taxi, the only operational vehicle on the street, and I took the elevator up to a studio where a plate of food and three smiling faces awaited me. We watched horror movies and drank seltzer by candlelight, even though the power grid for the building had held. The boyfriend left after dinner, lacing up his waterproof boots and wishing us all a safe night. The spouse and I blew out the candles and got into bed face to face, whispering and giggling while my new boyfriend, lulled by the sound of the warm conversation between his spouse and me, dozed at the foot of the bed like the old family hound. I woke in the morning wrapped in comfort and stitched into myself the memory of that joyful abundance of laughter in a full bed.

More recently, I fixed in another patch after waking up in the sheets of someone new who made me a beautiful breakfast: heaping pancakes with a homemade compote that minutes before had been a ripe mango in a sunny bowl. I ate while he lined me up in his sights.

"You're a hot fat girl with big tits and you have your life together in some significant ways," he said, watching me chew.

"I bet the men you date try to maternalize you, turn you into mommy for them. I want to let you know that I don't want to do that with you. We can figure out how to do something else."

I choked on the compote and my eyes flew open. He laughed and sent me home with a loaf of challah and a jar of seasoned butter. Bread and butter, as in, quotidian, as in, maybe, *Get used to this.* Or, bread and something salty, as in *lechem* and *malach*, the traditional Jewish gift brought to a housewarming, so that the newly established inhabitants might begin to sustain themselves. That night, ripping off handfuls of soft yellow bread, I thought to myself, *Maybe I have moved from wherever I was into a new home.* I held the feeling of a fist in my throat for a day and a half until the sound of the Rosh Hashanah shofar loosened it into sobs. When I laid my hands on myself that night, dipping under my hem to feel a fresh set of his fingerprints there, I touched something open and mended.

I'm still seeing that last guy, at least at the time that I'm writing this. Three months into dating, over bowls of steaming ramen, he told me in the contemplative, analytic tone he gets before laying out something devastating, that he understands why some people don't date fat people—because if they did, they would have to encounter and deal with their own fatphobia in their everyday life. It's just easier not to, he said, and there are social rewards for aligning with thinness.

"But," he said, "it's also true that most people are cowards. I'm here. And I want to work on that part of me, for your benefit and also for mine. Besides, fucking you is a joy."

My body registered pain, a pooling, burning panic, which sheared itself open and dissipated quickly, like he'd ripped through scar tissue. Then all I felt was relief. No one had ever been plain about their internalized fatphobia with me before, said the thing out loud that we both knew to be true. They'd glanced at it in fear, looked at it askance, but no one had been brave enough to talk to me about it. He asked me if I was okay, and I answered honestly. We settled up the check and walked together along Twenty-third Street holding hands and talking shit about James Bond, dodging drunk NYU students as they stumbled into the street in their makeshift Halloween costumes. When he fucked me that night, it was, as he had put it, a joy.

What else to do then but be brave and go deeper? I benefit from his candor and his frank assessments, which are sometimes bracing and hard to hear but scour out the bullshit and let me deal with what's actually going on. When my cat ate a rubber band and became constipated, he strode into a pharmacy and asked the employee at full volume for laxatives, and he didn't apologize or specify that they were for a cat and not himself; I found this to be unimaginably hot. I even let him put his hands on the part of my body that was red and angry from laser hair removal treatments, something that I could not imagine any earlier version of myself permitting. The version of me from five years ago would have sooner made up an excuse to leave his apartment before being seen or touched with an embarrassing rash for embarrassing reasons. Sometimes, I'm not even telling a story to him or to myself. Sometimes I'm just there with him. It is grown up and scary and exhilarating. It's both more and less potent than fantasy. It's real, and rather than being hurt or bored by reality, I'm practicing accepting this good thing in my life. The love I have chosen to give myself has allowed me to experiment with being loved by someone else, not as a fantasy or an archetype but in the full mess of my humanity.

Whatever the future holds in my relationships, whether with him, with someone else, or in a future that includes both him and others, I do not want to be a maternalized figure to my partners any more than I want to be an actual mother. Having PCOS is not why I don't want kids, I don't think, but it does help make the decision for me. While we don't know what causes PCOS, it's more prevalent in Ashkenazi Jews and might be the kind of genetic predisposition that intergenerational trauma hands down to people. Someone with ovaries is born with all the eggs they will have in their lifetime, all the theoretical chances for viability, for pregnancy, or for menstruation and shedding. It is Jewish of me to say it like this, but when months go by without a period, I feel pregnant with ancestors, with the mitochondrial history of an old country I do not know, wounds that are not mine, a language I do not speak. I am haunted by ghosts who wince at loud noises, who curse under their breath and stockpile food, as I stockpile body fat and as my irregularly menstruating body stockpiles eggs. The ancestors cling to my ovaries; if I do not conceive, my family line is ended, and when I die, I will take them all into the darkness with me, sinking the dreams they carried with them on the boat they boarded to arrive in America. We will go into the ocean together, a body of water governed by the phases of the moon, at the hand of my unruly menstruation that bucks against the regularity of the lunar tide.

My sea legs are hard won, so I make an effort to use them as often as possible. Whatever it means to glorify obesity, that's what I do for a living. Whatever that thing is that people are desperately afraid will happen if women do not put in the diligent work of hating themselves, that's probably something I'm getting paid for this weekend. I anoint my body with fragrant oils, with glitter. I nourish it from within and without, drape it in lush fabrics, velvet and sequin. I challenge my body with hard labor and reward it with hot water and soft sheets and the skin of others. When I perform, I am in the center of a stage alone, conjuring, inviting eyes to drink me in. People draw closer to me to tip me and I exhale a little more of my elixir. And every so often, usually at 2 a.m., when I'm dancing topless on the go-go box, my own hands and the hands of others roving over me, I am an animal again: an unkempt and unmade woman, unbecoming and un-becoming, peeling open the corners of my defensive layer with my fingers. I emerge, sluicing down the protective tents I've built for myself, chrysalis bursting midcreation, no longer woman but unrecognizable ooze, liquified pupa, a primordial ocean, big and beautiful, wet and new. On the very best nights, I let myself go.

Yes/No/Maybe

· ·

At the sex shop, I used to sneak lessons on communicating about sex into workshop curricula the way a parent might blend vegetables into a meatloaf. *It's good for you, but you won't reach for it on its own, so I'm throwing it in here and hoping you won't notice.* Anyone who attended a workshop also got a lesson in consent and negotiation, even if the topic that brought them in was butts or positions or aphrodisiacs. None of our customers would dare attend a full-length "how to talk about sex" workshop, even though at the grim, miserable heart of it, most other topics could be rendered irrelevant with effective interpersonal discourse in place. How do you play with someone's ass? Ask the person who possesses the ass in question. What positions are most pleasurable for me and my partner? Certainly a question it would be better to ask the person you're fucking. Which foods are sexiest? Well baby, which foods flare your partner's IBS? Okay, so not those.

One of the best tools we offered for facilitating communication was the Yes/No/Maybe list. This is a kind of inventory that features a bank of different acts, activities, roles, words, or scenarios. It is up to an individual to sort those items into three different columns. "Yes" means anything from "I love this, it really turns me on" to "I'm totally game if you are." "No" is no, full stop, and no one needs to justify why something is in their "No" column. That's for things you won't do, don't do, have zero interest in doing. Finally, there's "Maybe," to cover the terrain in between: maybe you would try this if you learned more about it first; maybe you would do this to your own body but you don't want to do it to someone else's; maybe you would do it in the rain, on a train, in a box, with a fox-tailed butt plug.

I filled out my first Yes/No/Maybe list during my sex shop orientation training, a personal sexual inventory. The queer, tattooed leather angel running my training recommended filling it out in pencil or making photocopies, because it was normal and to be expected that items would shift between columns over time. Sexuality is vast and preferences will change. If you're filling it out as a tool to use with someone, you can sit down together once your list is complete and go item by item. Nos are not wheedled into Maybes. Yeses and Maybes are compiled, negotiated. Since you are talking about acts themselves, you aren't talking about your relationship as the primary concern. Think of the difference between "I am not into being spanked" and "I don't like it when you spank me." Both may be true, but one formulation is more likely to result in hurt feelings.

This list is endlessly customizable and can collapse or expand depending on your needs. My favorite longform version of the list was created by my former coworker Bex, of Bex Talks Sex, and it exists online if you would like your own free copy.* Another co–sex educator of years gone by, Lena, had a great explanation of how the Yes/No/Maybe list framework could be used on the fly, in a quick negotiation with someone you just met in the cab from a party to your apartment: "I want to make out and jerk off together, but I don't want any penetration or oral. Is that cool with you?" Concise, efficient, fantastic.

Meanwhile, the audience at workshops usually balked and asked for shortcuts, for nonverbal tips, for ways to circumvent the need to talk to their person about what they are into. "But what if it's awkward?" they'd ask.

My initial confusion about this reaction gave way to obliterating sadness when I realized that most of our customers had never experienced enthusiastic consent before. People who think communication is not an important part of sex often pontificate about what they imagine is a dry, legal negotiation across a conference table: "My client would like to have access to your client's breasts for manual and oral stimulation. Are all parties amenable? I'm going to need that in writing." What that indicates to me is that they have never heard the wonder of, "I want you to tell me how you're going to fuck me with that strap," or "Look who just got all wet. Why don't you tell me about the fucked up shit that's got you so turned on?" or "My mouth is getting dry, babe. Can you get me some water so I can keep sucking that gorgeous cock?"

My all time, number one sex tip is that you really have to talk about things. Even if you think you don't. And you have to *keep*

---

*　Bex Talks Sex, "The Superpowered Yes/No/Maybe List," http://www. bextalkssex.com/yes-no-maybe/.

talking about things, because people and preferences change over time, and being conscious and checked in allows you to enjoy situations you'd never otherwise imagine yourself in.

For instance, I fell in love with a man watching him work a crowd of eight hundred people in Las Vegas at the Burlesque Hall of Fame Weekender. As he hosted, he used his long, lanky body for comedic effect, as a conduit for the boundless boyish energy that punctuated every punchline. The room was huge; it was the right size for him and for my inflating desire, which grew to crowd out even the most captivating showgirl's performance. I had seen something I wanted.

Fate booked us on the same 3 a.m. airport shuttle out of town. As the bus pulled out from one of Las Vegas's shittiest casinos, I looked behind me and saw him, awake, surrounded by unconscious passengers. We mouthed stage-whispered sentences to each other, and he asked to come sit next to me. We had worked a couple of gigs together before but hadn't spoken at length. I'd heard what I had needed from him to know that I was going to seduce him, but he didn't know that yet. The sleep deprivation worked its magic. Everything either of us said was funny. We waited together to check in for our flights, and we parted warmly on our way to our respective gates.

I made sure to stay in his orbit, which meant responding to his tweets and attending the shows he produced. He was more prominent in the burlesque world than I was, and I found that intimidating. A wrong move might mean losing the guy and my new, tentative foothold in the community. I did my research, read up on how he talked about himself. He was married but not monogamous. Sometimes, he'd tweet about being a bottom in bed. A cuckold, even, who enjoyed his spouse's extramarital relationships as much as his own. Okay, why not see if I could become a lid for that pot.

He coproduced a show of degenerate entertainment at a mishmash venue for out-of-towners and NYU students that exuded Midwestern man-cave energy, replete with mini-golf, a bowling alley, and an upstairs lounge with black leather benches and polished wood floors. I half-watched the show but mostly I stared at him in his suit. After the show, he sat down next to me and a friend, who had been the show's stage kitten,* and downed some champagne. This was my time to act.

"You were in my dream last night," I lied.

"Oh really? What was I doing in your dream?"

"It's embarrassing," I lied again. "It was a sex dream."

"Okay, tell me."

"I had dumped a cup of marbles on the floor of my living room. I was on my couch masturbating, and you were on all fours on the ground. I told you to pick up the marbles with your mouth and put them in the cup—and that if you looked at me, I would kick over the cup and you could start again."

"Oh my God." He took my hand in his.

I giggled. His face reddened and his expression turned serious. He slid down the leather couch onto his knees, crawled until he was positioned between my legs, leaned up, and kissed me.

---

* The term given to the fledgling performer who assists at a show by dressing up, looking cute, and picking up the stripper droppings.

He pulled a champagne bottle out of a sweating ice bucket and we passed it between our mouths and to my friend, the kitten, who sat beside me and leaned forward so that she could smother him in her breasts. He pulled away after a deep inhale, his eyes went rheumy with desire, and he asked me to slap him in the face. I did. He asked for it again and I hit him harder, holding the other side of his face in my palm, just like I learned from the sex shop's BDSM curriculum. We kissed again, deeper. We joined the other performers on the dance floor, fully debauched. His spouse emerged from the dressing room and jumped into their boyfriend's arms, wrapping their legs around him next to us, which really added something to the proceedings. When the champagne was gone, my friend and I slipped into the night air and stayed out gossiping until the sun rose over the French Roast on Sixth Avenue, where the handsome French waiter brought us tray after tray of free cakes and cocktails because we were, he said, *too beautiful.*

The emcee and I went on a proper date a week later: first a slow, winding walk through the aisles of Kim's Video, then what turned out to be a two-hour stress test at the worst open mic night Under St. Mark's had ever seen, and finally, a beer at some Irish bar. We stood on the curb in front of my subway stop and found reasons to delay our departure. I walked him four avenues out of my way to Union Square instead so we'd have a few more minutes. For the first time in transit history, my train arrived too quickly, and as the stale tunnel wind blew across the platform, we kissed goodbye.

Dating a married man meant it wasn't just the two of us making decisions about our relationship, which was both more and less straightforward than monogamy. After a frank negotiation at a Brooklyn diner where we set limits and established our safe word, a lovely onboarding e-mail from his spouse landed in my inbox. They told me they were excited to get to know me better and wanted to give me some lay of the land—they were the dominant member of the couple and so would do this communication rather than him, but the details had been agreed upon by both of them together. PIV* sex was the one thing off limits to us, they explained, and he didn't like blow jobs either. My heart sank. That was maybe 90 percent of the normative sex life of cisgender heterosexuals gone in an instant, evaporated from the jump. Which left . . . Fingers? Toys? Butts? Could a satisfying sex life be built on that alone? Still, what a gracious e-mail to send to the girl who wants to fuck your husband. I thanked them and we made plans for tea together.

I talked a big game to my new boyfriend, but I was twenty-four and completely green as a top. It helped that I was surrounded by sex toys and kink gear every day at work. The sex shop basement was a haunted tenement undercroft outfitted with peeling floor tiles. A pipe that was too hot to touch ran floor to ceiling, and next to it were the remnants of a display dildo that had melted on its scorching surface, nailed to the wall in warning. Most usefully, there was also a slanted, splintered bookshelf with sample copies of all of the books we sold. With my dollar slice or my dumplings in hand, I'd flip through the books in the library, reading as much as I could about roleplay, dominance, impact

---

* Penis in vagina. Welcome to this abbreviation.

play, anything I might be able to use with him. With my down time on Monday mornings, I'd practice my aim with leather floggers, striking the same spot of flaking paint on the wall over and over until I felt confident with my skills.

When it was time for me to make good on my promises of viciousness, I found myself pacing the block in front of his building listening to Junior Boys and trying to gather my nerve. I wore my Betsey Johnson halter dress that was covered in a pattern of silver screws. It snapped all the way up in the front, which meant I could rip it open at the right moment, and knowing I could deploy that made me feel sexy and powerful. Underneath it I'd poured myself into a bondage-style bra from Bordelle, the most expensive piece of lingerie I had ever owned, which I spent my entire Christmas bonus on during my first year of working at the sex shop. My black leather purse was full to the brim with lube, a paddle, cuffs, clamps, rope. Of course I overpacked. Was I going to top him with a tell—the way an American high schooler speaks French—too formal, too rote?

I pulled myself together enough to make it into his building and up the elevator. He greeted me at the door fresh from the bath in just pajama pants, his hair askew. I backed him up onto his bed and straddled him.

"Hi."

"Oh hi." He made a show of struggling to escape from between my thighs, but I felt his skin warming up with arousal. His big hands slid up my legs and gripped my ass. Every part of me was screaming out to fuck him. I felt a momentary pang—the sense that I'd met him too late, that I hadn't gotten to him first.

"You've got me trapped here, don't you."

"I do."

"And what are you going to do to me tonight?"

I rocked my hips back and forth a few times, slowly, like the churning of a ship at sea, listening to his breathing.

"Hmm, I don't know. What if we finally fuck tonight?" It was a bad joke. I knew it and so did he, but the insistence of my hips drove in the bitter notes of it.

"We can't," he said in a small grave voice. "That's off limits." His response flared a little anger in me, but the constraint was also a turn on. I have a lovely handsome man between my legs and I don't get to enjoy him fully—why was that hot for me?

"I don't know," I tried again, my tone sinking into a low purr. "The way we are right now, you can feel me, can't you?"

"Yes."

"And you can feel that I'm wet."

"Yes."

"And you can feel that between us, there's two flimsy little layers of fabric, and without those, you'd be pressed into my warm, wet pussy. And then we'd be fucking."

"Yes."

"Yes, what?"

"Yes, Mistress?"

"Boss."

"Yes, Boss." I raked my fingernails down the front of his chest, pleased at the pink zen garden lines that formed immediately in my wake. This felt like sexy improv, the back and forth of *complicité*, a rapport that builds through open communication between actors. He was my pathetic little bitch, sure, but he was also my scene partner. We were connected and present, and we both knew our roles.

"Now tell me, how good do you think this soft, tight, dripping wet pussy feels to fuck? To sink into it. To have to work a little to open it up even. How would that feel?"

"Amazing, Boss. Unbelievable. The best." I sped up the rocking of my hips.

"And do you think you'll ever get to find out for yourself? Do you think you deserve to fuck me?"

"No, Boss." The first rule of improv is to say "yes, and" to your partner, so that you are accepting the contributions they've offered and furthering things by adding details. But depending on the scene you've set up, the best way to continue in the reality of the scene is sometimes to say no. Our no was our yes, a continual reminder and enforcement of the boundaries and power roles we'd agreed to, a signal of our continued enjoyment.

"No baby, no. You don't deserve it. But tell me—do other men get to fuck this pussy? This one. The one that's grinding against this useless cock of yours as we speak?"

He squirmed and whimpered, his face and chest mottled with red and freckles like a Winesap apple. I stopped moving and gripped his wrists down into the bed.

"I think you need to answer my fucking question."

"They do. Yes, they do, they get to fuck you."

I tried not to sigh. I wasn't pursuing anyone else. I didn't really want anyone else. But imagining me with someone else—that was doing something to him that I'd only read about in books before, something magnificent to see. He was drifting into subspace, shrinking away into a limitless expanse, a floaty euphoria of adrenaline and endorphins. I kept my voice even and low as I reached underneath me and began stroking him with the tips of my fingers.

"Other men don't have to work as hard as you have just to get this. You take me out, you buy me dinner, all this time invested, all this fucking effort, and all you get is three of my fingers. Other men get so much more for so much less. Because unlike you, they are real men. You want to know the really unfair part?"

"What? . . . Boss?"

"Unlike you, they get to finish."

I slid my hand out of his waistband and tugged at my dress. The snaps popped open and the dress flew apart, exactly as I'd imagined. He gasped. My hand disappeared down the front of my panties, and it didn't take me long to find my own orgasm. I'd practiced with crops and paddles, but with him I learned that my words were my favorite tools for causing pain. Communication— hot. Go figure.

Despite, or maybe because of, the limitations, our sex life together was fun and interesting and stayed that way for the year and a half we dated. I try to imagine telling a workshop audience about our constraints. I didn't think there would ever be a way to convince the group that I could utilize the unsatisfied part of me to fuel my viciousness, and that it worked—for him, for me, a sea of yeses in our nos.

When we taught about the list, the teachers spent the least amount of time talking about hard limits, the Nos. That's because when the sex educators roleplayed a conversation between partners going through items on the list, we demonstrated that if someone said an item was a no for them, that was it. No debate, no pressure, no punishment, nobody talking someone else out of their stated limits. This was modeling, not as the world actually is but as we would like it to be. People's limits are pushed, ignored, and disrespected all the time, and it's awful.

I spent my junior year of college abroad in Prague, at film school. I should have been delighted over the sugar sculpture architecture, the crisp *pivo*—Czech lager that was cheaper than water—and a student body of international students, artists, and auteurs, eager to grab cameras and make cinema with me. But I wasn't. I arrived on a cold and cloudy morning and felt dull. I unpacked my suitcase and slept fitfully. The next morning, I awoke for orientation gripped with fever. I refused to miss class and so I spent the first week of school in a sweaty, medicated delirium. Something was amiss. It was foreshadowing.

The year I attended film school, the student body was a six-to-one ratio of men to women, something I was informed was unprecedented for the program (there were usually more women, they claimed). All of my professors were men, too, as were all the staff, except for one administrator and the woman who worked at the student café. The much-beloved equipment depot manager was a mouth-breathing fuckface (that's a film industry term) who wouldn't allow me to sign out any of the best lighting equipment but happily handed it over to any of my male classmates who asked. I'd stand at his Dutch door and ask again, politely, as he leered at me over the ledge, teasing: "You can have the HMI lights if you promise to act in a nude scene in my next project."

When 20 percent of the student body elected to write and stage rape scenes for a completely content-neutral directing exercise, I set up a meeting to express my concern about this trend to one of the school administrators.

The administrator nodded as I explained why the popularity of rape as a scene subject among my classmates was disturbing, furrowing his brow, affecting the sage noblesse of a golden retriever who has no idea what is going on. He leaned back in his chair and told me not to worry, that the school was founded on the belief that all students should be able to express themselves and make whatever kind of art they wanted. The school was not in the business of censorship. The guys devising rapes for the camera were just excited new filmmakers who wanted to make the most intense, extreme things possible as part of their art-making practice.

In my screenwriting seminar, we read Milan Kundera's short story "The Hitchhiking Game." It's a story about a couple that slips into a roleplay while on a road trip. The shy and chaste girl in the couple inhabits the persona of a wilder, sexually free woman whom her boyfriend has picked up on the side of the highway. The girl feels liberated by her new, confident self. At first her boyfriend is attracted to this side of her, but he quickly becomes repulsed and starts to punish her for not being the chaste and pure woman he thought she was. At the end of the story, he calls her a whore and tells her that he hates her.

In class, we analyzed the story and its themes. The other students talked about the importance of role and subjectivity in relationships, how we are all trying to be someone we are not, and how that hurts us all in the end.

I raised my hand and said something about how even though both characters lost their roles in the relationship, only one of them was punished for it, and wasn't that reflective of sexism on the part of the characters and maybe the author as well? In my memory, there was suddenly no oxygen in the room. My professor rolled his eyes. One of my classmates muttered, "Oh, a feminazi."

In the same screenwriting class, the following week, my professor said he was going to give each student individualized prompts for our next assignment. He went down the rows of students. "Try to write a scene with 50 percent of the dialogue of your usual scripts." He nodded, then moved to the next desk. "Focus on one character. Make your next short a study of a single person." He stopped in front of me. "You should avoid comedy," he said. "You rely on funny stories too much and I don't think that's your strong suit. Maybe do a romance."

We were split up into groups of five, acting as a rotating crew so that everyone would have a chance to do each of the relevant jobs over the course of the following two weeks: director of photography, directing, sound, and lighting. Depending on the needs of the production, people would double up in those roles or be cast as actors. The other four in my group were men: two guys from Denmark, one from Brazil, one from England. When it was my turn to act as the gaffer, a special request came in via a school administrator. The director of the project didn't feel like paying an actress and I was the only girl available. Even though I was supposed to be learning how to use lights, would I be willing to act in the scene instead?

I wanted to say no but I said yes instead. I was, after all, a team player. Not a feminazi.

I spoke to the director of the film about his vision. It was going to be very Hitchcockian, he said, with lots of light and shadows. I would play the heroine during a home invasion scene. He assured me the most intense thing that would happen to me is that one actor was going to put his finger in my mouth, and everything else would be handled through clever editing. I told him to make sure my costar washed his hands before.

I arrived on set, the director's apartment. We hauled equipment up five floors of a serpentine Czech apartment building. I was not as strong as the rest of the crew was, and I heard them sigh, caught beams of their disapproval. I was their dead weight. In compensation, I resolved to be the best Hitchcockian blonde I could possibly be.

I stood with the director outside the apartment door while he went through my blocking. Jiggle the keys in the lock, open the door, then look surprised by what I see. Then there'd be a cut to a reverse shot, with him filming on the other side of the door, POV of the invaders. All dark but, when I opened the door, a beautiful beam of light would come in. "Remember," he said. "Just look surprised."

He stepped into the apartment and called action. I twisted the key in the lock, opened the door, poured a butter-yellow shaft of light into the dark room. I looked surprised. My costar was standing a foot away holding a kitchen knife. He grabbed me and slammed me against the door.

The camera didn't cut. I looked surprised.

My back closed around the doorknob and the back of my head smacked into the door. I looked surprised.

My costar closed his fingers around my neck, pressing the knife against my cheek. I looked surprised.

The director called cut, and for a moment I thought it was an order to slash my face. Instead we reset the scene and did it six more times.

The thudding of my body against the door, the repetition of the knife in my face, had the equal and opposing effect of being lulled by the sound of waves. The terror came and kept coming, and it hammered me into someone who had the same shape as me but was vacant. The part of me that could leave left.

The crew set up for the next shot, the one where my costar would drag me to the bathroom. While we waited, he stayed in character to "get an authentic performance from me," jabbing the air near me with the knife while smiling and leering. The director called action. My costar grabbed me by the hair, had me suck his fingers, then rubbed my saliva all over my face. He slid the knife up my legs toward my crotch, the tip of the blade close to my underwear.

"Get up," he ordered. He pushed me against the bathroom wall and I heard the force of my body shattering the cheap shelving behind me, but I didn't register pain. Instead, I had a gauzy, distant thought: I'm going to feel this in the morning. Cut! The director needed a better angle, and we'd need to remove the broken shelving for continuity.

The crew member handling the sound stood grinning behind the director, looking into the viewfinder. "I guess she likes it rough."

Strange as it was, I started to laugh. I joked around with the crew. The director wanted me to cry harder, beg more, and I took his notes with diligence, breaking into choking sobs and heaving ragged breaths that snapped back into warbling laughter between takes. I ululated high and low like a starving baby bird. My costar and the director were really getting into it, and more ideas came to them in the moment, bursts of spontaneity. My costar pushed me against the toilet and the director loved it. So brutal! So gritty! During the next take, my costar pulled me down onto the floor and held my face against the linoleum, menacing me with the knife if I dared to get up. Technically, my far-off inside narrator chirped, this doesn't count as a rape scene. Cut. More laughter, big, percussive, abdominal laughs. I was not a feminazi. I was not the weak link. I was one of the guys. I was giving the best performance of my life.

The softspoken Danish guy who stepped in to do the lighting so I could be on the other end of my colleague's knife told the rest of the crew that the violence in the scene was too much for him, and he needed to go into the other room. He was nauseated.

"We're good anyway," the director said. "I got what I needed. That's a wrap."

I asked the crew if they would mind if I went straight home from the shoot, rather than dropping off the equipment with them at the media depot. No one protested. We packed the gear and brought it back downstairs to the curb and someone called a cab. "All set?" I asked as they turned away from me toward the taxi.

The tram arrived within minutes and I cried the whole way home.

Both of my roommates were home, as well as my friend Matteo, a passionate Italian boy who reminded me of a greyhound. They all saw my face.

"Hey, what the fuck happened to you? Are you okay?"

I sat on the couch and told them everything. Matteo's body stiffened in fury. He paced the floor between the couch and the kitchen.

"These guys are assholes! You need to tell the school what happened to you!"

"I don't know. Should I say something? Maybe they just didn't know how to block out a scene properly."

One of my roommates chimed in. "Hey, look, based on the theater acting I've done at school, scenes that are violent or upsetting are when the director blocks things out in the greatest detail, not the least. They need to know that they can't do this."

But it was the weekend, and no one was in the office, and I had to return to set the next day with the same crew. We switched roles to film someone else's project, but I'd been asked to act once again, so as a concession they let me help set up some of the lights before my scenes. As we prepped for shooting that day, I took off my sweater so they could see all the stone fruit bruises on my body.

"This can't happen again. I will walk off the set if I feel like anything even remotely like this goes on today. You really upset me yesterday and I didn't feel comfortable telling you in the moment. I am telling you now. This isn't happening again."

They offered me muffled, stilted apologies as we set up for the day's shoot. I grabbed heavy equipment, placed it where I wanted it, and refused their help. That day, my next scene partner, yesterday's lighting guy, needed to cry in a scene, so he watched the footage of me from the previous day to get into an emotional headspace. No one attacked me, and I ended the day too exhausted to speak.

Home again to my apartment in Vinohrady, while the sack of stones in my stomach clacked together. I took photos of my bruises and wrote to the school:

> Although I was the only girl on set, this is not the first time I have been in a male-dominated atmosphere. However, this is the first time I have felt uncomfortable and unsafe. I know I will be blamed by the other members of my crew for not saying anything at the time, but being physically and sexually abused in front of a group of men made me feel completely powerless. It made me feel useless as a person and a filmmaker. I am concerned that being female in this program is preventing me from learning effectively, and taking advantage of what this program promises to offer.

The same school administrator who had dismissed my concerns about the rape content asked me to meet again. I don't remember what happened in the meeting, other than that he asked me what I wanted to do. I don't remember what I said.

The men on my crew were not kicked out of school.

Each of the male professors I had that day opened their class session with a stumbling, awkward recounting of events as a preamble to a lesson about on-set professionalism, concealing my identity as if word hadn't already spread. The director of my filmed assault had edited the footage together and presented it for critique in his class. One of my roommates was in his section, and she walked out during the screening. In one of the other class sections, one of the male students who hadn't been there countered that "although it was probably assault, it wasn't sexual assault." My costar, the one who'd held the knife to my face and my thighs, responded to him with measured calm that yes, it had in fact been sexual assault. Another student said that since I was laughing between takes, I couldn't have been that upset or injured at that moment. Two students discussed how the director had had to use a real knife, how inconvenient it would have been to track down a rubber-tipped prop knife from the Barrandov prop warehouse, and how expensive.* Everyone had a white-hot take. Why didn't I run away? Why didn't I fight back?

One of my professors sent the class home early after his obligatory conduct talk—which became more of a rant, really, getting louder and angrier the more he spoke. As I packed my bag to go, he put his hand on my shoulder and told me that if anyone tried to touch me again, he would personally kill them. I nodded and felt no safer.

I stopped in the student café for a tea, where I was confronted by the film's director, the guy who over the course of several hours reviewed and edited together the footage of the attack. He screamed at me that he loved women and that now he was being labeled a sexist and no one wanted to work with him. He had just wanted my authentic reaction, just like Kubrick used to do with his actresses. He stormed off after I told him that I wasn't sorry he was having a hard time finding a crew.

---

* Renting a prop knife from Barrandov Studio for one day could cost up to $8 for a day's rental in 2020 and likely less at the time, accounting for inflation: Barrandov Studio, "Props Rental," https://www.fundus.barrandov.cz/en/pujcovna-rekvizit.

Don't worry. Nothing happened to him. Nothing happened to any of them.

The men on my crew were so upset by the slap on the wrist they received that the school considered them suitably contrite. I passed them in the hallways every day at school and sat in classrooms with the ones whose schedules overlapped with mine. In my acting class, I declined a trust fall exercise. When pressed, I said, "I don't trust any of you motherfuckers," which got a laugh. I stopped interacting with most of the people at the school, except for Matteo, my friend Ellie, and my two roommates. I did not drink Czech lager or visit castles or spend a weekend in Marienbad. I rushed home every night after class to sit with my knitting and watch *Grey's Anatomy*. Someone with my exact body showed up to class every day. My hands took notes and my mouth opened to laugh at jokes. I never learned how to properly light a scene. In the winter, my roommate, the theater actress, started hooking up with my former costar, the one who had admitted to sexual assault, so I stayed in my room a lot.

Rape became a meme at school. Pitches for more and more extreme rape scenes poured in, to the point where some of my classmates included rape in all of their assignments as a joke. My former director, the man who loomed over me in the student café to scream at me that he loved women, stood in front of the class during pitch day and proclaimed the twist for his next short film: one man was going to rape . . . *another man.*

When I finally told my mother what had happened to me over Skype, she flew into a rage, screaming and throwing stacks of phone books off the shelf. My father offered to get me a flight out of Prague with his points. *I want to stay in school*, I told them. If anyone was going to have their academic career interrupted or ruined by this experience it would be the men of my crew and not me. If they were staying, I was staying. If I was going to be a ghost, I could at least haunt the fuck out of these guys. These "artists," the men who sat in coffee shops opining on how best to light an actress's body for her rape scene, these visionary directors who did not trust their cast to perform adequately without being authentically attacked and traumatized, these provocateurs, these edgy and brave creatives, these enfants terribles—they may have pushed boundaries, but the boundaries they pushed were never their own. Rather, it was my body and my educational future that served as collateral, while the brave and terrible children gathered together behind the objective gaze of an expensive camera (one I was not given permission to use because I wouldn't show my tits), allowing the inert and distant eye of the lens to justify their enjoyment of my pain.

But when they could not shove a camera between us, when I encountered them on lunch breaks in the courtyard or passing through the halls of the school, these brave artists shied away from me with the elemental caution young village boys might exhibit toward a witch in the woods. My presence was damning, so I resolved to stick around to damn them.

My final project of the semester was a comedy, a guide for men on how to treat postmodern women, filmed in the style of a 1950s educational reel. I shot it at the school, with no budget, the shittiest camera in the equipment depot, and a majority female crew. At the program's graduation ceremony, I won the award for the best student film of the semester. A peculiar feeling washed over me. It wasn't pride but rather the sanguine pleasure of a kind of castration, the Final Girl grabbing the knife away from the killer after a protracted struggle, turning the pointed edge against him, and stabbing him, loosening his hot blood from his body in hammering sheets. The men who had humiliated me and hurt me could rent out all the HMI lights in the world and shoot all the rape scenes they could throw onto a storyboard, but I was the one in front of the school with the award and the accolades. Satisfaction, violent satisfaction.

When I returned to the States after school, I had a difficult reentry period. I made an appointment with my adviser to discuss what had happened abroad. He was reluctant to take the meeting. When I told him what happened to me, his face changed. He came near to tears.

"I had no idea. I thought you were just overreacting to some boys' club attitude. I'm so sorry."

I wrote a testimony of what happened to me to be included in the package that prospective film school applicants look through when choosing a program. Through a fluke in the university's housing lottery system, I was assigned a dorm room with a male roommate and didn't sleep there for a single night. I stayed on couches until I settled into an off-campus house with friends. The next guy I went out with over winter break fancied himself a dominant, and one night he locked me in his apartment to make me clean his kitchen as a punishment for not sleeping with him right away. I didn't date for a good long time after that. I graduated from college with highest honors in cinema. I still flinch when someone touches my neck.

I would love to follow this up with an uplifting postscript. I would love to say that I immediately got headhunted to start working at a film studio, and that the women I went to film school with went on to have incredible careers in the field. I would love to tell you that the men who had served as the crew quit the industry, each and every one of them. Maybe they got jobs in their hometowns and are living in their parents' basements, replaying their actions over and over again as if their memories were on a reel stuck in a projector, moving in the shadow of their shame.

But instead there's just a void. They are all blocked on my social media, so as far as I know they died, or they are famous filmmakers, or they're married with kids. As far as I know they're still punishing women for entering their artistic domains. As far as I know they still believe they love women. I remember all of their names except the boy with the knife's; his first name came back to me during a therapy session once, six years ago, and was gone again by the time I stepped out of the office. I no longer fantasize about murdering him, and the fantasy of forwarding him my psychotherapist's invoices has also receded.

My director wanted an authentic reaction from me. He got it. I got everything after, to carry with me, to pay for, to remember.

I remember picking up a video camera when I was eight or so. It was one of those big, clunky ones, roughly the same size—and with the same ease of use—as a living goat, that recorded directly onto a VHS tape. Two of my best girl friends from Hebrew school and I would get together after services and make videos. Any editing had to be done in-camera; we rewound the tape if we didn't get the shot. Any musical scoring was accomplished by holding my portable Discman up to the microphone. We printed out credits and used our own sleight of hand to create a constant scrolling effect by carefully sliding the pages up and off a music stand, zooming in until the lens blurred to smooth the transitions between shots.

We made dozens of videos together, everything from multimedia book reports for school to parodies of popular films of the day (*The Second Sense*: a story about a young girl who smells dead people—really rich stuff) to playing our own mothers. Three little Jewish girls hauling around a VHS behemoth, wearing our parents' clothes over our formal Shabbat service dresses, setting up shots and writing on the fly. We made these videos for ten years together. They became more sophisticated as we grew up, as technology improved. We obtained editing software. We wrote screenplays. We pulled from other genres, even going so far as to make a mockumentary retrospective of our own filmmaking careers. It was with those two girls that my love of film blossomed.

I don't make films anymore. It's a phantom limb. It's a piece of me that was cut off, but sometimes at night I still feel the impulse in me, a twitch, a flicker. I survived the horror film but I had to sacrifice something of myself to make it out. If there's a life lesson in this one, it hasn't made itself known to me yet. Until it does, it's just a wound of war, a place where the gash healed but doesn't look right.

•••

As I might say as a sex educator, the absence of a no is not a yes. We can pretend that the pain we cause doesn't exist in the time before someone says ouch. But the tree in the forest knows that it fell. And most of us acquire big hurts and little hurts and turn them into something else over time—a defense, a tendency, a quirk, a skill. Or they stay, oozing and open.

When I talk to audiences about consent, I tell them, *You get to have your no. Whether it's something you've done before and don't want to do anymore, or whether it's something you have no interest in ever doing at all. It can stop there. No explanation needed.* And someone in the crowd might nod, and I'll see in their face that they have sheathed the sword they'd drawn in their own defense. Like I said, in our workshops, we keep the "No" section short. It can split open with pain if we don't.

And so the sex educators move on to the third column, the "Maybe," after a deep breath. A Maybe can be a hopeful place. This final column is where the conversation gets going, because most of our lives occur here, the things we try out, try on, in the activities that make us curious or cautious. The maybe is where we stretch our understanding of ourselves. Being in my early twenties and working among sexually expressive people supplied maybe after maybe.

My first foray into the world of organized group sex was through my day job at the sex shop, working as the lube fairy at a 1920s-themed swingers' party. Someone had transformed a midtown loft space into a dubiously historically accurate fuck palace, with low music, lots of surfaces, and a generously stocked bar. Couples applied to attend, writing enthusiastic essays and appending sensual photos of themselves in hopes of being invited into the exclusive inner circle. I was there because I was banking the tidy sum of $13 an hour. I wore a cloche hat and a string of pearls to nod to the party's theme (my grandmother's! Oops, and thank you for your many sacrifices in war-torn Romania) and carried a variety of lubricants and safer sex supplies around on a cigarette tray. "Say, Herb, you're looking a little dry. Are you sure you don't want to moisten up?"

The floor of the elevator was embarrassed with rose petals, which bruised as the night wore on. Admission required a correctly recited password and participation in a welcome circle where men decorously avoided having to hold hands with one another because they were Very Straight. Nothing to worry about here, just Straight Men watching their wives get bent over velvet fainting couches by these other Totally Straight Men, watching their Totally Straight Dicks going in and out of their Hopefully Bicurious Wives. I was the fattest one there by a wide margin, and probably the youngest, too. In times of social anxiety I lead with my breasts, the part of my body that is allowed to be large. So I wandered through the rooms like a pneumatic Rudolph the Big-Titted Reindeer, my cleavage guiding my sleigh of condoms and dental dams from sex nook to sex nook. The glamorously leathery proprietress invited me to stay to play after my shift had ended. *Come play with us*, the Kubrickian beckoning. But I was twenty-two and freaked out and not attracted to these suited men and coiffed women. Nor was I convinced they were interested in a chubby Jewess with a newly minted film degree and a retail job, exuding as they did a vibe of, *We didn't pay $300 a head just to* *fuck the help.* I scurried into the subway afterward like a fallen woman. Didn't you hear? Hester Prynne lives off the L.

My *real* first sex party was later that year. I was asked to stage manage a private fetish-themed burlesque show that was the opening salvo to a play party hosted by an eccentric Australian tech-mogul guy who lived in Bushwick. The day was not erotic. I set up a stage, made playlists, and bought ice. I was jittery and so I confessed my ambivalence about the party to the event's coproducer. I told him I was afraid that the orgy would be a middle school kickball game, and I was going to be picked last. He laughed.

The performers arrived for their call time in leopard-print athleisure and hair scarves to protect their rolled curls. Our backstage was a bedroom, and the burlesque queens splayed out their lingerie and rhinestones on the bedspread. In the main space, a friend from college climbed up into the rafters. She was tied up in decorative bondage rope, and she go-go danced while guests filtered in. Darlinda, my newly self-appointed burlesque mentor, donned gold and silks and did an act as a genie, her lamp a Neti pot. She gyrated around a seated volunteer and, at the climax of the song, performed an enthusiastically wet nasal irrigation on her. Rosebud stripped out of a suit, smoked a cigarette and put it out with their tongue, stalked out into the audience, grabbed faces and made out with strangers. Velocity produced a butcher knife and, after stripping her clothes off, sliced at her breasts and vagina, fake blood freckling the first few rows. I was the clean-up crew, clearing costumes and body fluids between acts and setting the stage for the performers. Now I felt raw and real. I realized that there was little I liked more than wearing lingerie and walking around with purpose. I had begun to feel like I was good at both.

But would I go around the corner for the main event, the sex party? Rei, one of my sex shop coworkers, was also there just to see the show. We made small talk and nervously discussed the orgy. (This kind of conversation can happen when you're coworkers at a sex store. It is less okay when you work at, like, Best Buy.) We decided to be brave together. I told her I was going because a hot tub was promised. If nothing else, I could soak off a day of labor and corset-cinched bending and scooping.

The house where the party was being thrown felt like one of those Thai restaurants. You know the ones. Color-changing rainbow lighting, velvet wallpaper, a bar stocked with colorful bottles. Back through the first floor there were low couches lining the walls, mattresses on the floor. Further back, a fire-pit table, blue flames licking at the center. And further back, an indoor/outdoor hot tub. Downstairs, the serious fuck rooms, more mattresses, a wall of blue bubbles behind glass, a leather sling suspended from the ceiling, a shower with eight shower heads. It was a Bushwick-sex-party Polly Pocket, an unassuming shell of Brooklyn architecture with an entire world inside.

I stationed myself close to the entrance, where the organizers piled plates and utensils and platters of food. Who brought the egg salad to the orgy? I made a small plate of finger foods for myself and surveyed the scene around me. A guy approached me, a tidy man in his late forties with crinkly blue eyes and a shaved head. He set down a small stack of flyers in front of me.

"I'm Gabriel," he said. "I'm co-producing the party tonight. You should listen to this podcast I've been working on."

"Oh awesome, like *This American Life*?" I said.

"Yes, it's like that but with way more fucking," he replied. We both laughed and we chatted for a few minutes. He was playful and witty, and I was deeply grateful that this nice gay man would take time out of finding a man to have sex with to talk to me.

There were maybe seventy people there. This was not the same clientele as the swingers' party. There were people of different ages, maybe twenties to fifties, and representing a wide range of presentations. Tall, topless androgynous people with bleached hair. A short, muscular silver-haired man by the bar. A gorgeous, young, fat tattooed woman tied to a support beam. Unlike at the swingers' party, not everyone was white. People were fucking. Twosomes and threesomes splayed themselves across surfaces. Couples rolled on top of other couples accidentally, sending everyone into peals of laughter. People were fucking in all combinations of bodies and genders. The more I saw, the less important genitals seemed to me. I was too taken by staring at the faces of people caught in moments of pleasure. "This is so wholesome!" I exclaimed to no one in particular. A twink in a leash and dog ears popped his mouth off a cock he was sucking and looked over at me. "Really?" he said.

I found the hot tub, the most immediately compelling justification for getting naked. Gabriel was there, holding court and making conversation. He greeted everyone with casual comfort and familiarity, two qualities that were thoroughly evading me. He made me feel relaxed, and I adopted his tone of bemusement as we watched two bearded guys suck a gal's pierced nipples across from us. Together we pretended to be hosts of the world's worst talk show, holding invisible coffee mugs in our two hands, attempting to interview the nipple-suckers and the nipple-sucked. Ah, well, that's all the time we have folks—tune in next week to see if we get any of our questions answered. I looked down at my hands, which were pruning in the increasingly opaque water. "Okay, I think I need a commercial break," I said, moving toward the lip of the tub. I was so grateful to have made a friend, and I felt very lucky that there was still that part in me that can charm older gay men into taking care of me when I need it, and I felt that way until I felt two hands close in around my hips and pull me back down into the water. Gabriel's voice sharpened to a knife's edge. "And where do you think you're going?"

As it turned out, I had caught his eye while I had been stage managing the burlesque show—so I *was* good at walking around in lingerie! Gabriel was a kinky bisexual top who taught classes on all things BDSM. ("Mom, Dad . . . you're gonna love him.") I found out all of this at once when he asked my permission to spank me. That night he tore at me like he was trying to open a stubborn bag of Skittles in a darkened movie theater. He left me with bruises so severe that for the next week concerned women on the train were palming me phone numbers for domestic violence shelters. I wore the marks with pride. The violence was only one course of that evening's menu. We fucked downstairs against the blue bubble wall. It was enthusiastic, overwhelming, intense. The moment we finished, I remember collecting my thoughts and looking up, seeing that a small crowd of people had gathered to watch us.

I stayed at the party until dawn, and as the sun rose over the sex house, I suddenly became aware of each and every one of my pores. My coworker was still there, sitting on a couch, naked and grinning, blissed out. There were still some people fucking on the floor and on the couches. A couple of people were making toast in the kitchen. I went home as daylight roused the rats and cats of Flushing Avenue. I hopped onto the L toting my purse full of spent lingerie, and I sat in a subway seat facing a young couple and their kids, wondering if they could tell that my face smelled like balls.

When I went in to work my next shift, my coworkers informed me that Gabriel had stopped by to drop off his contact information for me. Like a fucking nerd, I wrote him an e-mail with the subject line, "Hiya, from your 'hot tub chum'!" I wrote:

> Just figured I should pass along my contact info as you did so kindly the other day. So glad that your inaugural event was such a success! By the way, my ass is vivid technicolor thanks to you. I'm using it to color coordinate my outfits.

His response arrived almost immediately.

> Thanks for the kind words. You're welcome for the colorful ass. I want to fuck your tight little pussy before the bruises fade. What's your day off?

Maybe I should not have been flattered by this. I blame it on a potent combination of being sick of dealing with passive ineffectual men and also being stupid and in my early twenties, which is practically the same thing. His directness worked. We spoke briefly of logistics, and then he sent this:

> Now that you're my girl, make note of a few details. You should always have Bulleit whiskey on hand. I'd prefer that you greet me nude with my drink in hand. You'll be left with marks unless I'm asked otherwise.

We began seeing each other once a week, exactly like that. Being submissive to this extent was uncharted territory for me, and I found a thrill in doing what I was told, being good, applying a stage manager's attention to detail. The ritual aspects appealed to me, and I wanted to be meticulous. The minutes before I expected his arrival were always nerve-racking: the correct timing on the pour of the whiskey, so as to not erode the ice and dilute the drink; when to take my clothes off; the sudden strangeness of waiting naked in my own apartment, opening the door without clothes on (also known in some counties as Landlord Russian Roulette). But I did exactly as I was instructed, the right amount of whiskey with the right number of ice cubes, every time. I'd hand him the glass and we would kiss hello, then he would sit on my couch while I knelt at his feet, untying his shoes for him. We would talk and giggle for some time while he held a fistful of my hair in his hand. And then he would signal that it was time, and then I was under his command and did whatever he wanted until my alarm rang, at which point it was time to get dressed and go work some retail.

This was my Monday afternoon for about six months: whiskey and ice and shoelaces and bruises. Sometimes I brought new toys home from work for us to try. A couple of times he brought friends to join us as a surprise: once a boy he thought I would like, and once a married friend of his who liked to pay to watch. (That encounter broke my IKEA bed—splintered wooden slats, a job well done.)

And then one Monday he arrived later than planned, and so we didn't have the full two hours we usually set aside to fuck. It was early May, gray and rainy. We were both feeling tired, so instead of the whole routine, we lay in bed together, listening to folk music and watching the rain. I was naked, he was clothed, and he had his arms around me. *This is not love*, I thought. *I will never love this man. But this is intimacy, and this is exactly what I need right now.* My alarm rang. I had a work call to make and he had business elsewhere to attend to, but he told me to be his date at a podcast taping downtown that evening. This was exciting. I could be an obedient chew toy and a smart and fully actualized person and someone's date all at the same time. I don't remember what I wore out that night, but I know that I fretted over it and that I looked great.

I was a couple of minutes late for the show and by the time I arrived, the seats in the front were all taken. I saw Gabriel at one of the cabaret tables near the stage. I sat toward the back at the bar, waiting to get his attention. Finally the show announced an intermission, and I watched as he walked toward the main entrance at the back of the venue. On his way out, I grabbed his shoulder to get his attention. He looked up at me vacantly, eyes glassy and red from drinking, and made a "Wh—" shape with his mouth. He looked through me for a moment, as if I were an apparition, then he turned and walked out of the venue. I waited a couple of minutes to make sure he was really gone, really not coming back for me. Ouch. I grabbed my purse and got out of there as fast as I could.

I was gutted and bewildered. The same man who had just that very afternoon held me tenderly in his arms did not recognize me six hours later. Summoning optimism, I sent him an e-mail with my favorite folk song from our day together and asked him what had happened. I was hoping for some kind of exonerating explanation. You see, that day there were brain parasites loose in New York City, and one had control over my body, so I was being programmed to make it back to the hive before dawn? I'm actually a spy and there was a mission going on that I couldn't allow you to become part of? I waited for a response. A week later while I was at work, my phone buzzed. A text message from Gabriel. Finally, the answers I sought. He wrote:

What day next week are you going to suck my dick?

I felt the way it feels when a middle school dance is over and the teacher suddenly flicks the lights on in the once atmospheric auditorium. Oh! He probably has no memory of that night. Oh! This man is an alcoholic. Oh! You didn't know that because you see him in the early afternoons before he gets sloshed. Oh! The whiskey ritual means I am paying for his drinks. Oh! Maybe it's not a great idea to fuck men in their forties who are free Monday afternoons when you're not sure what they even do for a living.

The following Monday, he came to my apartment. My clothes were on and I offered him no whiskey. We sat on my couch and talked. He told me that that night he'd been drunker than he had been in years, that he had no recollection of seeing me there at all, that he was sorry. I think I said, "Thank you for your apology," and, "I am not going to fix this for you, but if this is a problem, I hope you get the help you need." He asked me if I would continue to play with him, and I told him that I did not know. We both fidgeted and struggled to get our bodies in a comfortable configuration now that I was not sitting between his feet. I faced him, faced away from him, tucked my legs underneath myself, even straddled him for a few moments for a fleeting, awkward kiss. But I was not his submissive anymore. I was not his ragdoll or his girl or his target practice or his date. That door had been padlocked shut.

Stories from real life don't end neatly with a pithy sentence or a full stop unless someone dies or enters witness protection. We're both still here. We've seen each other since at other orgies (running into a former flame at an orgy—is there an agony aunt for this?), at parties, and it's always okay and warm and brief. A few months ago, a burlesque producer posted a photo of me on Facebook to advertise an upcoming show, and under it I saw Gabriel had commented, "I love her."

I sucked my teeth. Ah. Looks like he recognizes me now.

Dear readers, a coda: I severed the umbilical cord that had connected me to the sex party house in the winter of 2014. I had found other orgies, and I'd gotten turned off by this one's slow descent toward Burning Man–fundraiser efforts and the hipster racism of parties that encouraged feather headdresses or Silk Road–inspired garb. "What's next month?" I bitterly muttered to a friend as I pasted myself against the velvet wallpaper. "Africa? Why not invite people to come fuck about the entire continent of fucking Africa?" That December, the party theme was "XXXMas." I stayed home—too Jewish for this shit—while Rei attended (she had become the Australian guy's tenant and felt obligated to go). While mingling, she started chatting up one of the only other Black women in attendance, who revealed to her that they were both dating the same white guy, which he had conveniently failed to mention. Rei called me from her room, where she was hiding, crying. In the background I heard the unmistakable thump of an EDM bassline. "I feel like shit," she told me. "I feel worthless and I hate him and there's too many white Santas fucking downstairs. I'm scared because I don't know what I'm going to do tonight. I feel like I want to die."

I asked her to stay on the phone with me while I hailed a cab. She packed a couple of her things into an overnight bag and I had her breathe in and out with me over the phone. She stayed in the room where she was hiding until I confirmed that I was right outside in the car. A few moments later, the front door of the house opened and I caught a gust of the party. White bodies in cheap storebought red and white costumes, fake marabou trim, crushed imitation velvet, swarming like insects. An elf in green and red bent over, getting spanked in the hallway. Grinning sweaty white men with gleeful erections poking out of their red trousers. The briefest glimpse of hell itself. And, parting the red sea, Rei in a faded gray sweatshirt and jeans, anguished and in a full run toward the cab. I opened the door and she slid into my embrace. That night she slept on my couch, and in my head I built a pyre, a burning man, and heaped into it the party invitations, the condom wrappers, the texts and phone calls, the Santas, the party store costumes, the men I had fucked who had not deserved it. Finally, I initiated the immolation of that girl in her early twenties who wasn't sure that anyone would choose her at the orgy.

I'd written my Yes/No/Maybe list in pencil for a reason, and through the violence and wisdom of experience, I rearranged my columns. When we awoke, Rei and I sat in the living room together, and in the tradition of women who deserved better, we sifted through the ashes of the night before in the light of a gray morning.

Work Nights

· ·

My friend Tiger Bay and I talk about some burlesque gigs as "family nights" and some as "work nights." A family night happens when you glance at the booking confirmation e-mail and see the names of your best friends on the lineup with you, or even people you're less close with but you still like and respect. Some people are fantastic to share dressing rooms with. They are on time, they bring snacks or gossip, and they do their fair share of the work. Most of the time, those same people are also excellent performers, because they're practiced, self-possessed, and stress tested. You know a night with them will be fun and easy; the sound system could be on the fritz, the audience could be hostile, but it does not matter. You weather the storm with family. And the good gigs, with family, don't feel like work at all so much as a party occasionally interrupted by performance duties. On some nights, the party keeps going after the backstage clears out, and we spend our wadded-up tip money on late night pierogies, tacos, pizza. We can more or less shut down a restaurant that way, laughing and shit talking, shoving too many people in a booth next to our suitcases, still in our show makeup. Burlesque performers are good tippers and excellent company. Going home with money after an incredible night feels like cheating.

And then there are work nights. When the lineup is mostly brand-new girls who don't know the ropes and need a lot of reassurance and help, that's a work night. When you know that you're going to have to carry the whole show yourself, that's a work night. Or when you're backstage with a veteran performer who tends to overdrink and corners you while you're trying to get dressed to complain about her love life, you're working the whole goddamn night. When someone in the cast is complaining nonstop about their body, when people start leaning out of the dressing room to assess which audience members they're going to try to fuck after the show, when it feels like you're trapped in an elevator that's rapidly losing oxygen with someone who would be better served by dialectical behavioral therapy than a booking, you walk away from the show feeling burnt out, your body heavy as bronzed baby shoes, ready to quit altogether.

Any performer who has been in the business long enough has had a few truly miserable nights. At the first show I produced, I arrived at the venue to find diners mowing down steak salads on the back patio, where the performers were supposed to put their things and change. The venue owner suggested that we could get dressed out there anyway. When I explained why it was a bad idea to have people changing in front of his patrons, he said he would see what he could do. He disappeared and returned to tell us that he had found a different space for us: a crawl space up a ladder. I was green. I could have said no, and I didn't. The performers

I hired bravely changed in the crawl space and teetered down the ladder in their gowns and heels to perform. The bathroom didn't lock, so a startled patron got an impromptu private piss show from yours truly. When Tangerine Jones took the stage to read a collection of the catcalls she had received, a man from the audience began shouting at her, harassing her about how she was making up the harassment. When he started moving toward the stage, I signaled to the bar's security to get him out, and to my astonishment, they shrugged. So with the mic in one hand and the sleeve of the man's shirt in the other, I pulled him from the bar and onto the street myself. The cast and I still shudder when we talk about that night, but all of us are still on speaking terms, and that counts for something.

Was that worse or better than the god-awful gig in Memphis when the venue's website, its social media, and our own flyer each had different showtimes listed? Our audience was already seated and ready for curtains up when we arrived to load in, and they had to wait two hours for the show to start. I bought them all a round of drinks while they waited for us to get ready. It wasn't that generous of me. There were only four people there. We needed each and every one of them to stay. That wasn't even the most sparsely attended show I've done. I lost parts of myself that I won't get back at a performance during the coldest night of the 2014 polar vortex, peeling off my clothes at a weeknight bar for an audience of three. There were more people in the cast than in the crowd, and I cried backstage thinking about having to take off my winter layers. We each made $7 in tips.

When I told some of my performer friends that I was going to write about the worst gigs I've ever done, they each assumed

I was thinking about a different one. Oh, you're going to talk about the Marina Abramovic performance art tribute you did where you almost got murdered? No, it's not a fun story and I've mostly repressed that one. Oh, another said, this is going to be about the time you were covered in breast milk and inadvertently got electrocuted when they brought that Tesla coil onstage, and everyone saw the bright blue bolt of electricity zap you and the crowd gasped and the show kept on going? Weirdly, no, still not my worst, I don't think. I survived, the gig paid well, and from what I heard, I looked cool getting shocked.

Emotionally withholding fathers would describe these experiences as character building. I learned from them: confirm with the venue where the backstage will be before the show, double and triple check the start time of the show on all marketing collateral, perform for three people as if they were three hundred strong, and make a striptease number that allows you to retain a fur coat for as long as possible. And, uh, don't trust your audience to lead your performance art. And check if there's going to be live electricity if you're going to be onstage wearing something conductive. The worst, the truly worst, were the gigs where I didn't learn at all, or at least where the takeaway was not worth the personal suffering.

About a year into my tenure as a burlesque performer, I was contacted by a newer, controversial producer to do a show for more money than I had ever made as a fledgling art stripper. "It's like burlesque, but in 3D!" he repeated throughout our conversation, as if the other kinds of burlesque happen via line plots or graphing calculators. The third dimension he was referring to was mess. His concept was to hire three burlesque performers to each do the three messiest, most in-your-face acts they had. The venue was a heavy metal bar in Brooklyn. "You can even make more money if you do lap dances after the show!" he crowed.

I was booked alongside Ula Uberbusen, a good friend of mine from the sex party world, and Apathy Angel, a take-no-shit contortionist showgirl. Ula and I were the first to the venue. The bartender seemed to be the only person who even knew the show was happening in the first place, and the producer was nowhere to be found.

Apathy arrived maybe a half hour before the show was scheduled to begin. She had just been robbed and was missing the iPod with her music on it and some of her costume pieces.

"I don't know what the fuck I'm going to do for three acts when I don't have costumes or music," she said.

I shrugged. "Just the fact that you showed up is already above and beyond. I mean, the producer isn't even here, so I don't really think it matters. Just do literally whatever you want for a couple of minutes and you can call that an act."

Ula offered up some songs from her iPod and the three of us put together the show order. We waited twenty minutes more for the producer to arrive, which he didn't, and then we started the show on our own to little fanfare. In case you are picturing a stage at this venue, let me assure you that there was none. Rather, there was a small, rickety platform that I think had been stored in one of the broom closets; it was set up against the back wall of the bar, right next to the bathrooms. It was the size of two apple boxes pushed together and about as sturdy. I thought of the producer's words to me on the phone: "This crowd loves to get fucked with! Don't be afraid to really get in their faces!"

Whose faces? The crowd consisted of maybe ten grizzled trucker dudes experiencing varying levels of intoxication and interest in the painted showgirls in front of them. Ula worked her way through her program with grace. Apathy improvised beautifully, even finishing one act by slinking over to the bar, sitting down, and slamming a shot (thus cementing my lifelong professional respect). And I did my best. My final act of the evening was my fully nude act where I pour hot candle wax on myself to a Radiohead song, the emotional indie strains of which I hoped wouldn't get me booed out of town by the metalheads in the audience. I walked into the room to murmurs of conversation, but by the time I hit the "stage," all eyes were on me. And when I dropped my silk veil covering, revealing my entire naked body, a 350-pound trucker seated not six feet away from me bellowed with gusto: "I'M NEVER GOING TO FORGET YOU!" The feeling, ultimately, was mutual.

Halfway through the show, the producer showed up, wasted. He stepped in to host the show, making rude comments about us, our bodies, and what we would be willing to do for and to the audience members after the show. He crawled around on the ground like an animal. He took his clothes off and tried to insert the microphone into his ass, a piece of outsider art perhaps. Apathy, Ula, and I stood with our arms crossed against one of the walls, waiting for him to stop.

"I wish he had just stayed home," Apathy said.

The show ended with a whimper as the producer rambled and promised that we would be dancing on the bar, which we all declined to do. I packed my bag in the corner and watched a pantomime unfold across the room between Apathy and the producer. She said some words to him as his body crumpled in defeat, and I watched as he took out his wallet and started making piles. Apparently, he had tried to pay her less than he had promised, so she made him empty his wallet and divided it evenly into thirds, which she distributed to Ula and me.

"He didn't produce the show, we did, so why should he fuckin' get paid for it?" she said.

After the show, I realized the reigning international queen of burlesque had snuck into the audience that night midshow, on tour from Australia. She sat toward the back of the bar with a couple of my friends, but the lighting was so low that I hadn't noticed them at all. They gave me a ride home, and I stewed in the backseat in humiliation. Later I heard she'd specifically asked to see a real shitshow, nothing refined, so at least she got what she wanted.

It makes me uncomfortable when people make assumptions about why I perform, particularly when they tell me that I must do so as a confidence booster. The statement is a projection of their experience; they watched me do something that to them requires self-assurance, something they could not imagine themselves doing, with all their hang-ups and self-consciousness. And so, they extrapolate, this must be some kind of Ouroboros, a triumphant experience which feeds back into itself, enlarging my power. The truth is stickier than that. It doesn't matter how I or any burlesque performer feels about themselves on any given evening. We are hired to take off our clothes, so whether it's a good brain day or a bad brain day, whether we love our bodies or despise them, whether we like the audience or hate them, we are at work, doing our job.

Some nights threaten to undo any personal work I've done, scattering years of therapy sessions like glass pebbles from a smashed windshield. Early in my hosting career, I was emceeing on a lineup with an insult comedian. His schtick was that he provided the voice for a puppet of a sentient blunt, which someone else operated on stage while he bravely sat in the back of the room and made fun of people. During his set, he turned his attention to me and said, "Fancy Feast, when you heard that to do burlesque you would need a bra and pasties, you must have heard a pie and pastries." The audience murmured, shifted, laughed in discomfort. He rattled off a few more fat jokes and then switched gears to show a video of the blunt puppet doing street interviews that I couldn't hear because I'd started to dissociate. It's a neat trick that happens when things get really bad. Some part of me goes, *Okay, let's get out of here*, and the dipped-in-ice-water, lung-crushing, tingly extremity panic is replaced by a floaty, bubbly calm, like I had just huffed some nitrous and was now kicking back and enjoying the sensation of my brain cells dying. But I couldn't stay gone, because I was hosting the show. So when he was done and it was my turn again, I tried to calm my wavering voice as I outro-ed him on the mic.

"Give it up once again for the last living California Raisin! Or whatever that was. Gorgeous construction on that puppet. And while we are here, let's give a shout out to iMovie, for making it possible for anyone, absolutely *anyone*, to make a movie." I got a laugh, thank God, and when I went backstage to recover while the next performer was on stage, the comedian leaned into my personal space, glowering.

"That was fucked up of you to say. You really ruined my set."

"Oh, I'm sorry," I remember responding. "I didn't realize it might not feel good to have someone saying mean things about you on the mic. I can see how that might throw you off. It's hard to perform when someone says rude shit about you, huh."

I stared at him, furious, until a clown (an actual clown performing in the show, not this fool) stepped between us to break it up. Whatever I got paid for that gig was not worth it. I thought about the blunt puppet the next time I performed the same striptease I had done that night, and I hated him and myself for it. I will no longer perform in shows with insult comics. The juxtaposition between the clenched defensiveness of insult comedy and the inclusive celebration of burlesque is like a mouthful of toothpaste and orange juice. These are the kinds of standards I get to have now, ones I never thought I would need to develop but that the industry necessitates, much like my "don't date any more magicians" rule. Didn't think I would need that one, but adulthood can yield life lessons in a lot of different ways.

It took me some years to realize that the work night / family night distinction is, like most binaries, false. Some nights will bring immense frustration in the company of dear loved ones, while others will be unexpectedly sweet and divine thanks to unfamiliar company. And still others will be so absurdly, insanely stressful that they'll turn colleagues into cherished allies. I don't believe that the only way to make friends in the industry is to be mutually compressed into diamonds of anxiety, but it's how I got close with several of my best pals.

One spring I went on tour with three other performers, starting in Savannah, Georgia, and working our way north to New York. The crew was Tiger Bay, whom I still only knew from afar at that time; Evelyn DeVere, a gothic romantic performer and seamstress living in Charleston; and Porcelain, a sex-kitten performer and model from Seattle. Porcelain and Evelyn were complete strangers to me. Tiger had tapped me as an emcee for their three weeks of tour dates after their previous host had fallen through, and I had always wanted to perform on the road. The four of us packed our gig bags and clothes and toiletries and merch into Evelyn's stick-shift sedan and charted a meandering course around the East Coast. Our first Saturday night show was in North Carolina, at a small venue on the side of the highway of the type that I have drunkenly referred to as a "racist hookah bar"—not because I've necessarily observed anything overtly racist but because it's the kind of bar that's populated and staffed by white people, and if anyone who culturally grew up smoking hookah walked in, they would probably get the stare-down from the patrons. The kind of place with a blonde belly dancer. Lots of white people with dreadlocks eating crumbly hummus and doing fire poi out back. You know what I mean.

The owner of the place greeted us warmly and showed us to the backstage area. It was small, which was not a problem, but it was also flooded with about an inch of stagnant water shot through with live electrical cables like so many venomous snakes, coiled to strike and on standby to electrocute us all.

"Not sure what's going on there," he shrugged. "So I guess try not to use too much of the floor."

We hung up our costumes on exposed pipes and put on our makeup in the small hallway behind the curtain. Once again, there was no stage to speak of, just a carpet that marked out our territory for us to perform floor-show-style. The audience facing us was rabidly drunk, which we were all used to and comfortable with—after all, we would rather perform for vociferous barflies than weird, judgy folks on their phones. But one of the patrons had brought a bag of whistles and distributed them to the rest of the crowd. At uneven intervals, a high-pitched shriek would cut through the Saturday night din and jolt a showgirl's hand, wielding lipstick or a mascara applicator for that last minute touchup.

"Can you ask the audience not to blow their whistles during the show?" I remember Evelyn asking.

"Of course, and it fucks me up that I even have to say those words," I replied.

The show we brought on tour was a little bit of everything. Evelyn's acts were masterful pieces of classic burlesque in gorgeous handmade costumes. Porcelain was pure sex, moving naturally and sensually through her acts. Tiger did two pieces, one imitating a popular animated fish from a [litigious company's] feature film and one as a BDSM cyberpunk superhero with a baseball bat. I was hosting the show and performing one act, a comedic talk-and-strip recalling Gypsy Rose Lee and the earlier days of the form.

Here is what the audience took away from the hour and a half long show: Tiger Bay had a rhinestoned turtle appliqué on their crotch. How do I know this? Because every time I went to introduce the next act, they would yell, "Turtle!" or "Bring back the turtle!"

It's not my job to tell the audience what they should enjoy. Whatever the takeaway is, fine. If a couple of people really get it and understand what we are trying to do, that's great. If we make women feel more excited about their own bodies or more generous about other people's bodies, great. If people like watching folks wear shiny things and move around, great. And if people cannot get enough of a crotch turtle, then . . . fine.

Words that I had to say on the mic: *Please, don't blow whistles at the dancers. I know you're all very excited about the turtle. The turtle is not coming back out.*

The flood backstage had taken its toll on the sound system, which pumped out only tinny and treble notes. We all missed our cues, attempting to count ourselves in with no bass rhythm to cue us, bumping to musical stings that simply were not there. What did come out was just the vocals, so we stripped to what sounded like an underwater coffee shop singer-songwriter showcase. Porcelain got stuck in her corset, and she cried backstage in the flooded dressing room after her number, fearing, with complete inaccuracy, that she was the deadweight of the show.

We slogged through the remainder of the acts and then set up our merch table of jewelry, pasties, Polaroids, and lingerie and mingled with the audience. One guy waved me over to his group.

"Hey! Can you take a photo with us? Would we need to pay for a picture?"

Typically, on the road, yes, but I didn't feel like haggling. "No need to pay me. Let's get a good photo!" I stepped into a group of nondescript white guys who put their arms around my shoulders and we posed.

The guy with the camera lined up to take the shot. "Okay everyone, say, 'Republicans are the best!'"

Holy shit, what? My smile faltered for a moment, and I heard the shutter click.

"Ha!" the man said happily. "I figured you would hate that."

"Oh! So why did you do it?" I asked in my syrupy customer service chirp, and then I stepped away in disbelief.

Nearly simultaneously, a man walked up to Porcelain with his girlfriend on his arm. "It's SO NICE to see girls with SMALL BREASTS on stage. You know, I ACTUALLY prefer ones like THAT—" He jabbed an index finger at Porcelain's chest. "See my girlfriend?" He pointed at her breasts. "Hers are BIG. But I like 'em more like YOURS."

The girlfriend executed a lobotomized laugh. "Yeah, it's true! Mine are too big for him! He likes small boobs like yours!"

Elsewhere in the room, a woman stared down Evelyn, her eyes scanning her entire body. "How *old* are you?" she asked. Evelyn told her, and she smiled in relief. "Oh good," she said. "Never mind then." Yet another man approached me near the stage area. "Hey! I just wanted to say that, you know, no offense, you don't usually see—you know, I mean, I have a friend who is not that confident in herself, and she's also . . ." He held his hands out in front of himself and widened the distance between his palms, expanding, puffing out his cheeks like the blueberry girl from *Charlie and the Chocolate Factory*. *Oh my God, he's trying to come up with a word that means fat that isn't fat.* I decided not to help him find the word, and so he didn't. We stood facing each other in our personal wilderness while he slowly inflated until one of his friends standing behind him rescued him.

"Curvy!"

"Yeah! She is curvy like you, and boy, you don't really see a lot of people like that who are feeling good about themselves. It's really something!"

"Yeah, I wonder why that is. Excuse me." I walked away to join Tiger Bay at the merch table.

Just then, a woman approached Tiger. "I really liked your second act; that was so hot. But do you know what would make it better?"

I need to pause right now to talk to you about that sentence. No performer, no artist, wants to hear that right after a show. That's not to say we refuse critique. Any artist requires a healthy amount of peer review to innovate and create work that is compelling and rigorously considered. What I mean is, we don't want to hear it from the drunk woman who just screamed "turtle" at us for an hour and a half. Nor from anyone else who is unaware that, if you saw it on stage, there's probably a reason for it. There is a reason for every costume piece. There is a reason for the choreography. There is a reason for the music choice. Burlesque isn't art by committee, and at the end of the day, it reflects our own individual worldviews. Basically, the moral of the story is, shut the fuck up.

Tiger steeled themself in anticipation. "Uh, what?"

"I think it should be to a different song. You know that song that goes, 'I wanna fuck you like an animal'?* I think that would be much better."

Tiger's face grew tight as if they were being Botoxed from all sides. Their body language was stiff, and they dismissively raised one hand.

"Ok. I'll change it."

They drew their mouth into a wide, wan grimace and held it until the woman walked away. Tiger started breathing again once she was out of sight.

Later that night, as we counted our money and traded stories, piecing together the criminally terrible events of the evening like Rashomon, we laughed until our obliques spasmed. And critically, we came up with our signal for when one of us needed rescuing. If we asked each other, "Hey, is it time?" that was the check in to see if we should separate the performer from the situation they were in.

This signal served us well over the next three years' worth of tours—because yes, there were more. It was time when someone paid $100 for a Polaroid of all of us nude together with him and then wouldn't leave the backstage.† It was time when Porcelain's ex showed up unannounced to our show and wouldn't let her end

---

* The song, "Closer," is an excellent one, but it's overused, trope-y, and expected in burlesque at this point. Plus, it doesn't match the intention or mood of Tiger's act, which is more rooted in cyberpunk and is deliberately unknowable, rather than being something familiar you can sing along to.

† He told us he was going to "break his dick off" to the picture when he got home, but when we saw him in his car outside the venue after the show, he said he hadn't been able to wait and had just finished jerking off, and when I tell you that Tiger Bay ran screaming into the night like a cartoon character, well, I half-expected a Tiger-shaped dust cloud to be left in their wake.

their conversation. It was time when Tiger wanted to spend the night with an audience member who had just been screaming at her girlfriend outside the venue, and the rest of us physically dragged Tiger back to the car. It was time when the polyamorous Burning Man couple letting us crash at their place texted Porcelain to invite her into their bed that night (she chose to remain sleeping on the beanbag chair they had provided). It was time when we opened for a ska band and one of the members of the band talked at length about punching a refrigerator because his girlfriend wouldn't "shut up about feminism." In our subsequent years on the road together, we've grown to be seasoned stage veterans, but our safe word has stayed indispensable to us. Burlesque will always provide an ample amount of wild stuff to contend with. With all of the unknowns that we face in any given show, it could always be time.

Evelyn, Porcelain, Tiger, and I have stripped together in deplorable conditions, in smoking venues off the highway in North Florida's meth country, in deserted drag clubs where territorial local queens ousted us from the dressing room, and at a diner in Alabama where the show was a total surprise to the patrons. The sedan has broken down, we've gotten lost, and we've slept on too many couches that were more cat hair than fabric. But as long as we are performing together, damn it, it's family night.

Walkaround Gig

· ·

Rich folks pay fabulous people to dress up in themed looks and stand around at their parties. No shit. It's known as walkaround, and it's one of the most coveted gigs in nightlife. The other word for a walkaround gig is *atmosphere*, which captures the ambient nature of the work. If you're hired to work atmosphere, you're not doing an act on stage; that draws too much attention. Rather, you've got a gimmick, a character, a prop, a trick, a live animal, that you use to interact with event attendees, and then you move on. Walkaround means offering people the lowest-possible-social-stakes way to mingle; we're there and gone because we have to work the room, and we're paid to be friendly. Think Bar Mitzvah entertainer, or Renaissance Faire wench.

Atmosphere performers set the tone for the night and provide plausible immersion for whatever mood the host is trying to create. Sure, you could throw a Versailles-themed party in your hypermodern Flatiron loft, but wouldn't you evoke France more convincingly with the presence of powdered courtesans in panniers and wigs giggling behind fans and gossiping about the aristocracy? If you're going to be a crashing bore and throw the four-millionth fête that willfully misinterprets the thesis of *The Great Gatsby*, don't you want flappers with rolled-down stockings and dresses they didn't buy from Amazon who actually know how to Charleston? Of course, not all themes are quite so obvious. I spent one Halloween doing atmosphere in the VIP room of a warehouse party in Bushwick, receiving sinners' confessions and letting patrons drip prayer candle wax on my breasts. I was hired to write and distribute love notes at a private soft-kink art party. Some wealthy client saw my photo and insisted that I drift through the halls of a Manhattan supper club for a Prohibition-era haunted circus soirée. I don't make this stuff up; I just go and report back.

Atmosphere work requires less energy for a more sustained amount of time. A four-minute stage performance is all adrenaline, fast and furious detonation, and it's done in a mere breathless moment. Walkaround requires social stamina, but it also lets you stand enigmatically next to a staircase for half an hour in silence and consider it time well spent. It's paid dress-up for the amusement of the affluent, which means a few hours of being gawked at as the most fascinating creature on the planet by some of the most boring creatures on any plane of existence. The wealthy folks who have had all the excitement of being alive ironed flat by money and privilege walk away with an "experience," and you walk away to the subway with an envelope of cash. Everyone gets a peek at everyone else, and isn't that why we go to parties?

Walkaround work is not as abundant as it used to be, for burlesque people anyway. Perhaps the rich are doing something else now, something I'm not invited to. Circus and sideshow talent is still getting occasional party work, but even some of that is drying up, and a big check at the end of an easy day of walking around with feather fans now exists mostly in memory. Believe it or not, burlesque used to be part of the pantheon of corporate entertainment, most often for hotels, restaurant groups, and other segments of the entertainment industry. Those jobs involved showing off in a boa and headdress, maybe removing a garment or two, and generally ending up mostly clothed for ridiculous amounts of money. God bless the girls who got that work, but they didn't tend to hire fatties, so I never got a piece of that particular pie anyway. The loss of these kinds of jobs isn't just budgetary. Cultural tastes have changed. Legitimate concerns about inappropriate sexual behavior in American workplaces has meant that even the most liberal business ventures have returned to team morale building at campground ropes courses, fitness cult seminars, or whatever. I have never worked a corporate job so I don't know the HR take on this, but it feels like sex these days is off the menu. I was never jazzed at the idea of horny events people did with their coworkers at normie jobs (I must have sold one too many dildos to a mid-level executive for an office party Secret Santa swap), but I do know that I started my career fielding frequent requests for corporate gigs, and then at some point, they stopped. I could be pedantic and attribute this to the #MeToo movement, which created visibility and accountability for inappropriate workplace sexual behavior, but that doesn't feel accurate. There's altogether less space for open sexual expression, in every slice of American life, and so what does trickle out is shunted into private spaces, or transmuted, displaced, projected elsewhere.

A few years ago, I was hired for a walkaround gig at a private party in Midtown. The backstage dressing room was a tiny L-shaped hallway by the service entrance, lined with cinder blocks and mirrors tipped over on their long side. Performers crouched near the floor, putting the finishing touches on their makeup. I squatted next to my backpack, slathering glitter lotion on my tits. The door next to me opened at various intervals, and startled Jazzercise students from the adjoining dance studio filed out, muttering soft, sweaty apologies as they tiptoed through naked bodies to the shared exit.

"The evening has two parts," the producer called out to us from the joint of the L. "The first one is more Bosch, okay? More earthly delight. So just greet the crowd and play with them and keep it light. Just before midnight we'll do a big reset and come back out for the second half, which is going to be more of the deadly sins and the, you know, the consequences. The dark side of indulgence. Okay? Any questions? Great, let's get some people who are already in costume out on the floor and set, and doors for the guests are in ten."

My outfit for the first half of the evening was chosen to evoke Bacchanalian excess: a gold fringe belt, iridescent pasties, a voluminous purple feather collar, and a big cascade of curls, topped off with a handmade rhinestoned grape-and-vine headpiece. I wandered out into the party space, night-and-day different from the cramped backstage. Pink and blue lights shone down through tastefully tangled vine latticework. Fog was pumped in. The sound system played nondescript, bassy techno music. I chose my area and sat my bare ass on the long and well-appointed bar. An assistant handed me a silver tray and several bags of grapes. I piled the grapes onto the tray like an old master setting a still life and curled my body around them, framing the platter with my hips.

The guests began arriving. Most made a beeline for the bar. Tickets to this event, I had learned, were $250 apiece. The people who bellied up to the bar, who bellied up to me, were mostly guys in suits, rich but not attractive, rich in the way that replaces attractive. By their side were women, well-dressed but not happy, well-dressed in the way that replaces happy.

I was hired that night to portray gluttony. The producers hadn't wanted to tell me that outright: *Hey, fat girl, can you play the* grosso *sin that is mostly about eating too many snacks?* They had approached me with a respectful but vaguely apologetic tone, stopping short of saying the sin itself, so I was the one to speak it aloud. When I heard how much they were willing to pay me for the gig, there was no question in my mind.

So I invoked gluttony, hedonistic excess. I laid on the bar and held clusters of grapes against my face, occasionally sucking one into my mouth and popping it between my teeth. I let my gaze rest on the guests' faces. Several approached me with their phones, wanting to take a photo of me feeding them for their Snapchat feed. I sat up for the pose, had them position themselves so their back was to me and I was behind them with my legs straddling them, my bare belly and bush brushing against them. When a man wanted me to feed him, I held the back of his head as he ate, gently instructing him how wide to open his mouth for me. And when he asked to feed *me*, I looked at him the whole time and concluded by thanking him. With women, I let them do whatever they wanted. They could just eat it off the tray if they preferred (People get shy! Maybe she just wants fruit without the experience!), or I could feed them, or whatever. People came back for seconds and thirds.

Two guys stayed by my side for my entire first set. The shorter and handsomer of the two guys got flustered when I spent too long interacting with another guest.

"Oh, I'm sorry darling. Am I making you jealous?"

"No, I'm not jealous. I mean, I have a girlfriend."

"Well then, I guess it's a good thing you never had a chance of fucking me anyway." I winked at him. He clicked his tongue.

"I have to ask. What's it like being hot and naked for a living?"

"Boring. Why don't you buy me a drink?"

His friend handed me a long-stemmed vape and called me Goddess. I pretended to be tired of the attention and told him to go away and report back on what he saw in the other rooms of the party. Between chats, I looked around and watched rich people get hammered on top shelf vodka sodas. I watched folks do fat rails of blow off their iPhones. I watched two or three people at a time hop into the single stall bathroom next to the bar.

I started feeling pleasantly high from the vape. The taller guy brought me a drink. I set it behind a planter without drinking any of it. The producer came and grabbed me.

"You should take a break! Go have some water and relax."

I sat backstage and tried to take a flattering photo of myself. Too much overhead light. I looked at myself in the mirror. I didn't know what Goddess those guys had seen. I felt hopelessly human, and looked it, too.

"You're a hit! Are you having fun?" The producer handed me a bottle of water. "It's almost midnight, so if you would like to transition into the second look of the evening, now is a great time."

I had been told to take costume inspiration from Hieronymus Bosch's painting *The Garden of Earthly Delights*. But everyone is naked in that painting, except one big bird man who's eating, I think, a person. So I hadn't packed anything to wear for my second look. All of a sudden, I regretted the cavalier choice. Naked looked way too naked. One of my friends was backstage, and I flagged her down.

"Hey, do you have any extra rope lying around?"

She handed me a thirty-foot skein and I tied a basic *karada* body harness on myself to make my nudity look less accidental, fixed my hair in the mirror, and then headed back out into the party. The second half of my set was floating atmosphere, meaning that rather than having a station, I was doing walkaround between the different rooms and floors of the space.

Do you know what it's like to be the only naked person at a party of a hundred strangers? It feels like you didn't read the RSVP instructions on the invitation and now you're in a Hawaiian shirt at the Oscars. And it's a nightmare to slide through masses of people, to interrupt conversations, to fear, even irrationally, that your pussy is going to make a snail trail on someone's Paul Smith suit as you scoot past them. What's it like to be barefoot at a party where everyone else is in shoes, and they're drunk, and they're spilling their cocktails and worse? What's it like to be the only fat person in the building? I wanted so badly to crawl back up onto the bar, where I was comfortable, where I could see over the crowds of people. But barefoot and fully naked and just clearing five feet tall, I felt incongruously and improbably invisible.

For this set, a producer had handed me a big round cake, dripping with custard and topped with chocolate ganache. "Hi," I cooed as I walked by people, "would you like a bite of my cake? I promise it's delicious."

You would have thought I was walking around the party with a loaded gun. My nudity was not offensive to the partygoers, but the cake was obscene. The cake was a big red pulsing butthole on a platter, a baked Piss Christ, a chocolate cartoon bomb from the ACME corporation. People actively shooed me away.

"I'm on paleo."

"It looks great, but no thank you! Too much sugar."

"I'm drinking my calories tonight, babe."

"Oh my God, I can't. I'm doing a cleanse."

In the murky basement of the sin-themed party, two feet from another atmosphere performer, who was locked in a cage, screaming obscenities at a gaggle of onlookers, was a drunk man explaining to a naked fat woman in a rope harness that he is trying to eat less gluten. Someone nearby offered to eat the maraschino cherry off the top. I felt like screaming. *You rich pieces of shit would snort rails off a puke-encrusted toilet seat but you're drawing the line at a fucking chocolate custard cake?*

I felt dejected, and the mood in the room was changing to that surly, restless kind of drunk energy, the moment when the low pressure hits and the clouds wait to unclench their torrents. My body sent me the signal to bail on the basement, so I headed back up to the main atrium where I had started my evening.

I spotted an unoccupied leather chaise in the back corner of the room. Nearby, another performer sat on a podium in a pig mask, admiring her own reflection in a mirror. Okay, I thought, this is as good a place to set up shop as any. I reclined on the chaise and took a fingerful of the cake, scanning the room for receptive eyes as I ate. The cake was delicious, and the first couple of mouthfuls transpired in complete anonymity. I felt, for the first time that night, like a voyeur. But one of the men who had stayed with me at the bar turned and saw me. His eyes lit up and he walked toward me.

"Can I eat some cake off of you?" Ah, so I'd broken the seal.

He dug his fingers into the cake and spread it across my neck and nipple, then slowly sucked it off. I closed my eyes and tilted my head back in mock arousal, wondering how much of my body glitter he had consumed. He slid down to the floor onto his hands and knees.

"Thank you. It is an honor."

As he slunk away, I returned my attention to the dessert. By this time, several people had taken notice of me and were standing in dumb transfixion, their eyes shiny and focused on the slow descent of my fingers first as they plunged into the cake and then as they rose again to meet my open lips. I reacted to each bite with focused pleasure, digging my nails into the flesh of my thighs as I ate, furrowing my brow, letting my fingers rest against my mouth for a few extra seconds. I curled my toes, twisted my neck, gathered a fistful of curls, and pulled my hair from my face.

More and more and more people began turning around, nudging their friends, stopping in their tracks to watch me eat. Sometimes I would pause just before I took a bite, just to see how long I could drag out the anticipation. A man in a suit had started to sweat watching me. A straight couple followed every move of mine with their eyes, settling into a full-bodied experience of transference, eating through me, shuddering upon the completion of every swallow. One woman stood ten feet away from me, the next fattest woman in the room, a woman perhaps fifty pounds lighter than me but still too fat for this party. I held her gaze with mine, tilted my head, and let a big wide smile break across my countenance. She smiled, too, shaking her head.

A guest who'd been brave enough to heed the event's dress code adjusted his black feathered wings behind his suit, sat next to me on the chaise, and offered me some cake in his open palm. I bowed my head in benediction and ate the cake out of his hands, taking his fingers into my mouth.

"Holy shit."

By then a sizable group had gathered around me to watch. I felt giddy and strange. Were these people thinking about feeding me or feeding themselves? Were they thinking about fucking me or being me? Did someone just realize they had a feeding fetish or a thing for fleshier women or women in rope, or was it just this singular moment that we were all in together, where I was enjoying my body—this thing they have learned to be afraid of— and food—this thing they have learned to deny themselves—and

I was embracing them and it and myself together, folding their desires into each fingerful of the dirty cake I ate, absolving them of their sins by taking it into my own body. I was consecrating the profane, the things they have taught themselves not to enjoy. Their no met my yes, my indulgence, my gluttony, my abundance, the reality of my body, my mouth—a mouth they coveted; a mouth they wanted to possess, to kiss, to feed, to fuck; a mouth waiting to receive them, selfless in my greed, bottomless in my appetite, hungry.

I watched a group of people get turned on in front of me. They watched me and I watched them watch me. I floated back into my body and realized that I was full, that I was empty, spent. I stood up and swiftly carried the cake out of the room. Several men followed me back toward the dressing room.

"Come back! I'm ready to feed you!"

I shut the door behind me and sat on the ground, gulping air and water. I felt floaty and nauseated from the sugar and endorphins. The moment the cast was released for the night, I put on my street clothes, stuffed my makeup into my backpack, and disappeared into the night air.

You know that uncanny feeling you get when you see a photo of an event you witnessed and you go, *No, that wasn't it*? I saw a photo of myself at the party, and I believe it happened, but it didn't resemble my memory. I saw someone lying on a chaise, but it wasn't me. It was a fat girl tied up in rope, belly hanging over to one side, smiling up at a man in black angel's wings seated next to her. Not me, not how it felt, too tangible and too tawdry, too much light from the flash making the leather upholstery look shiny and cheap. This happens every time I see a still photo of me in performance. Who is this motherfucker and where does she get off doing my act?

A month later I got a phone call from a burlesque producer in the Hudson Valley. "So I read a thing on Facebook about you getting naked and eating cake at a party. Would you be interested in doing that again?"

Not a breath escaped before I said yes. We don't get to choose our legacy, or the psychic baggage that other people ask us to hold for them, but I could do far worse than being the fat girl who gets paid to eat cake at parties.

Mistress of Ceremonies

· ·

The first words out of my mouth on the mic are, "What's up, motherfuckers?" because "motherfucker" is a gender-neutral alternative to "ladies and gentlemen," and I don't want anyone left out of the filth. Hire me to host your next event: your wedding, your kids' b'nai mitzvah, your husband's wake. Your function will be inclusive and smutty. And as much as I love doing my prewritten bits, presenting the material I've worked in front of crowds and hammered into anecdotes and tactical turns of phrase that I know will land, the truest flex of my prowess working on the mic is how quick I can be when someone puts me on the spot. That's when the audience sees my talent, the speed of my response—when I'm out on a limb with nothing but my experience to lean on. That verbal tightrope is my happy place because I've got a mouth on me and I like finding out where it will take me.

I befriended the only five burlesque performers in all of North Dakota when they heard about a show I was producing and hosting in Manhattan called *Now You See Us, Now We're*

Drunk. The name and premise were lifted from a tradition in my college improv troupe wherein the improvisers would perform a show, do a bunch of shots during the intermission, then attempt to repeat the show verbatim. For the burlesque equivalent, I asked performers to bring their most technically challenging acts, to be performed twice, once sober and once sloshed. A nerdcore rapper performed an ever-accelerating version of Johnny Cash's "I've Been Everywhere" while lashed to a chair, attempting a Houdini-esque escape. Two showgirls presented a duet of synchronized choreography and multiple handstands, while another did a reverse strip, cinching herself into a corset. Iris Explosion, a goofball genius performer, assembled an entire Mousetrap board game layout from pieces stashed in various parts of her costume, running the "mouse" through the course as the coup de grâce. The show sold out, and bodies crammed the back room of the dingy bar, straining to get a look at the inevitable chaos.

A midtier beer brand sponsored the event and donated several cases of cans to be used as a raffle prize, which the veteran producer who had mentored me early in my career drank most of during the show. His decision to drink outside booze nearly got us all banned from the venue, except that the show had done so well for bar sales that they let it slide with a stern warning. In the morning, my phone was cluttered with texts from members of the cast pledging sobriety, and others from performers asking to be booked the next time I did the show.

Weeks later, I got a Facebook message from Oopsie Daisy, the producer of the Blue Belles, the sole burlesque troupe in the Roughrider state. She asked for my permission to use the theme for their own show in Fargo. I responded by saying sure, and thanks, and that I wished I could be there to see it. She wrote back to ask me if I wanted to come out for the show, and I told her without hesitation that I did. She told me not to worry about navigating the airport because it was "just one room," and that I would know who they were when I arrived. Which was true, of course, because even out of drag, a plainclothes burlesque girl is conspicuous. When I got off the plane, I spotted a group of girls in leopard print leggings and winter boots who greeted me with a cardboard sign bearing my stage name. They whisked me straightaway to the Northern, a strip club in Fargo where mixed drinks were $5 and they featured a brunch buffet show called *Legs 'N' Eggs* on the weekends.

The Fargo gals innovated in ways that massively improved *Now You See Us, Now We're Drunk*. The venue was a real, gorgeous theater that seated 350 and boasted an expansive backstage. The producer brought a Breathalyzer, so that each performer could blow onstage and have their blood alcohol level read aloud to the crowd. The drunkest person onstage that night would receive a loaf of bread as their prize. To prevent drunk driving, they secured sponsorship from a party limousine company, who would be chauffeuring us to and from the gig. All of that and they donated proceeds from the show to an animal shelter. These broads, man. To show that I could really hang with the Midwesterners, I blew three times the legal limit and blacked out in the limo home.

The following year, in the summer of 2016, the Fargo girls asked me back to reprise the show at a motorcycle rally. I did not hesitate. The event was held way out of town, so I hitched a ride with Ophelia Flame, a Minneapolis-based performer and longtime club dancer who had performed in the Fargo show. She packed keto-friendly weed fudge in her travel bag and talked me through the basic language and culture of MCs, or motorcycle clubs, as we barreled down the highway. "Colors" referred to the insignias on the leather jackets or vests the bikers wore. The top rocker, the patch just underneath the back of the collar, was the name of the club, and just under that I could find the club logo or image. Underneath that was the bottom rocker, which designated a territory, city, or location where the MC was based. On the front of the jacket, I could find the wearer's rank or title. Uninitiated and new members of MCs were called "prospects," and they needed to be deferential to more senior members of the club.

I was told to avoid one-percenters, the bikers who sought distinction as outlaws and who were more likely to be affiliated with white supremacist hate groups or to run drugs and be involved in sundry criminal activity. I could tell who the one-percenters were by looking for a patch reading "1%" on the front of their jackets or vests.

I told Ophelia I was scared, and she waved a dismissive hand in my direction. "You'll be fine. This isn't Sturgis, dude. The guys in Prometheus MC are lovely people." I did my best impression of someone whose fears were assuaged and nodded.

We parked at a Pilot Travel Center for coffee and played a round of Big Buck Hunter in the arcade. Land yawned out in every direction. The road told a meandering story in repetitive, reshuffled billboards for Christ, Arby's, Christ again. We turned off the interstate, the only car to enter Wahpeton, a town named for the Lakota Sioux word meaning "leaf dwellers." The 2010 census put the population of Wahpeton at 7,766. There, the Bureau of Indian Education operated the Circle of Nations School, which was originally established in 1904 as the Wahpeton Indian School, an assimilationist boarding school where students were punished for speaking their native languages. I know all of this because I was frantically researching the town on Wikipedia, as if I could learn enough about my surroundings to become someone or something else.

We passed knee-high corn fields, white silos, scrub trees and ditches and squat farmhouses. The terrain was pancake flat, ironed smooth by the pressure of lumbering glaciers of bygone millennia. Air and dirt and crops and nothing. Ophelia pointed to an outcropping of trees and we drove up to it. White clay kicked up in the air and tinted everything with haze. White semis were parked in a line near a front gate. Behind them, a line of tents and RVs dotted the main drag on one side. On the other side, red picnic tables clustered near a white wooden building, upon which hung a painting of a chubby nude brunette petting a pig with a Harley-Davidson tattoo on its ass, along with the words "THE HAWG TROFF - FINE EATS." Ophelia off-roaded until she found the Blue Belles' RV, and we parked next to them on the grass. The RV was stocked with water and groceries for the weekend and, most crucially, featured a toilet. Sharing a Porta Potty with several hundred bikers is one of Dante's lesser-known circles of hell. I'd rather be picked to pieces by harpies, thank you very much. I watched as two groups of bikers played tug-of-war with a length of rope while, inexplicably, an iridescent peacock strutted across the campsite. Off in a nearby field, the female bikers and the male bikers' "old ladies" competed in a keg toss game, hurling the barrels shot-put-style, for distance.

As soon as I put my bag down, the Blue Belles began assembling for the first of our weekend appearances: the bike wash. Most of the riders had already shined up their motorcycles in anticipation of the event, but as for most events with bikini babes and hoses, the stated goal was not the point. I put on a black two-piece swimsuit, black boots, a denim chambray top, open and tied under my tits, and big gold sunglasses, to mask the fact that I didn't want to put on eye makeup.

"I'm worried they won't like Jews," I said to Anytime Jones, one of the Belles.

"Well, I'm a little freaked, too. The Black lesbian and the Jew can stick together, Fance," she said.

We joined the rest of the girls out in the field where bikers had begun to gather. I didn't know which parts of the motorcycle were supposed to get washed, so for the first bike or two, I stuck to safe bets (wheels, mostly) and chatted with the bikers. How many times had they attended the event? Where were they coming from? Were they excited for the show? Everyone was convivial and kind, which people tend to be when your breasts are out. The Belles and I made sure to spray each other with the hoses, to bend over more often than necessary, to otherwise fulfill our womanly duties.

Once we'd worked our way through the queue, we were released from our duties for the day, and we shifted into show prep. The RV transformed into a backstage area as the Belles wiped the dirt off their knees with baby wipes and donned sequined gowns and feathers. I'd brought a straightforward striptease act with a long dance break in the middle, during which I exited the stage to interact with the crowd. Usually when I perform this act, I hop in people's laps and beg them to motorboat me, or I lean over a table and shake my ass in their faces. This time, as my heels scraped along the concrete seating area, the bikers backed up, refusing to interact. I was worried they hated me until I heard the applause at the end of the number. After the show, one of the members of Prometheus MC thanked me for the performance.

"You don't see a lot of strippers who look like you."

"That's right," I said.

"You really did your thing out there. I respect the hell out of that. I think the guys were surprised you came out into the crowd. It takes balls to be out there."

The man made my night—my God, a fan. I went back to the RV to change. I sat on my bunk bed, scrubbing off my makeup and staring out through the dingy window as motorcycles rolled past.

"Open your mouth."

Sin Sear, the baby of the group, was standing over me grinning.

"You want a chocolate?"

I opened my mouth and she popped one in.

"Weed fudge?" I asked, chewing.

"Mushrooms!"

Oh, I thought. *Good.*

As night settled on the campsite, I ate a burger at the Hawg Troff and waited for the shrooms to kick in. Biker dudes and their female company mingled, pouring liquor into plastic cups and sitting around campfires. The late-night entertainment was a rock band playing covers, fronted by a guy with shaggy hair and tight leather pants. In the middle of a lovely conversation about life in New York City with a biker named Slim, over a trash can fire, my brain irised out like the end of a Looney Tunes cartoon. That's all, folks. I could no longer speak and the gleam from the fire had begun to morph and undulate. I looked over at Oopsie Daisy, who had also had one of the chocolates, and she smirked as if to say, *Yup, me too.* She and I peeled off together to explore the outer edges of the camp. She collapsed into the grass, laughing, and I joined her, stretching out to watch as stars and planets pinballed before us. Oopsie grabbed my hand and tugged me along as we exited the campsite, skipping down the center of the empty highway.

She wanted to keep going down the asphalt road, but the neighboring wheat field was calling out to me, so I veered into it instead. I was alone. The moon hung low just above my head, a creamy, radiant disc. It kissed the shimmering tips of the crops, which shifted and bathed in a phosphorescent glow. The night air rustled the wisps of wheat, the sound of a million purred secrets. The sky was the darkest, freshest blue, stretched beyond any conceivable limit, alight with a fusillade of stars. The soil below me was still radiating the warmth it absorbed during the day, and the rich petrichor smell of June earth and the wheat and moon and sky thrummed together, a nocturnal song that vibrated in my ears and fingers. The night was open and I opened with it.

I wanted to sleep out in the field, but Oopsie spotted me, and we walked back to the RV together, shuffling into our bunks, the last girls to sleep. My bed rocked like a ship's cabin. If shrooms were open to accepting notes, I thought, I would thank them for their great work and then suggest that they not last for five hours. Sleep eventually won out. In the morning, I awoke to the PA system playing the national anthem.

Saturday morning was the big ride. I'd spent the night communing with a wheat field while the other girls were finding bikers to ride with, so all of the bitch seats were taken. Riders, colors resplendent, drained out of the campground and onto the highway until the site was still and quiet. I used the down time to take a bird bath with a water bottle between the campers, using a giant Confederate flag hanging nearby to towel off with. I got dressed and had a long chat with the pitmaster as he prepared a whole pig for the barbecue meal that evening. Ophelia's biker came back early, so she and I drove into town for coffee and indoor plumbing, and then to the dingy town zoo, where we caught up with some of the bikers who'd stopped there to see the animals. We came back to camp in time for pulled pork sandwiches as the riders trickled in for dinner, then we started the show process all over again.

Saturday night's show was the reprise of *Now You See Us, Now We're Drunk*, and I was the emcee. Right before my ascent to the raised platform of the stage, I looked over at the already wasted sound guy, who had searched in his iTunes playlist for "Gorge Thorogod." My arrival on stage was greeted with the familiar applause of the liquored masses. Wikipedia research could not help me here—but it didn't matter. The audience, like most large groups of gathered drunk people, was ready for a show. For the fluffed and feathered burlesque ladies and the rough and ready

MCs, throwing our clothes on the floor was our own open road, and the more I dug into that feeling, the more I felt our two groups stitch themselves together. The Black lesbian and the Jew included. It felt like the stuff of miracles.

I got bold by the last act because I knew I wouldn't be introducing anyone else to the stage, so I offered a five-minute window during which time anyone could bring something to the stage for me to drink. The DJ played "One Bourbon, One Shot, One Beer" while bikers bum-rushed the stage with bottles of Jack and Fireball and vodka in plastic jugs and moonshine and cracked cold beers. I had some sips of all of it. Memories from then on are hazy. I think one of the girls, at some point, got stuck in a tree, and I think some bikers acted as volunteer firemen to catch her when she jumped down, or fell. I sobered up in Ophelia's tent that night, smoking joints and listening to the late-night musical guest, another rock band. The special effects guy went for broke with the fog machine, hammering on the smoke release button with the frantic commitment of a man held at gunpoint. The breeze pushed the thick, rolling green troposphere back behind the stage and into our tent. I lost Ophelia, who was sitting two feet away, and she lost me. Cutting through the dense brume came the voice of the lead singer. "This one's for YOU, OBAMA!" The band kicked into CCR's "Fortunate Son," unaware of any political irony, and Ophelia and I dissolved into peals of laughter.

Sunday morning had the somber wistfulness of the last day of summer camp. There was a church service that I didn't attend. I looked around for one of the stands selling commemorative merch so I could get a T-shirt, but they'd all packed up. A grizzled biker with a ZZ Top beard who'd just loaded his motorcycle into his white semi spotted me standing on the asphalt where the merch tables had been. He grabbed his own rally T-shirt from the cab of his truck and handed it to me, refusing all protestation to the contrary. I thanked him and packed the shirt away with my wigs and gowns. The girls and I kissed and hugged goodbye, and Ophelia dropped me off at the airport on her way home.

Burlesque can be a passport and a permission slip. It's a reliable way to see things and go places I never would otherwise. I keep expecting enemies and making friends. I have to assume that's white girl shit. Privilege. I'm grateful for this kind of range and access. It still feels surprising.

Four years after the rally, I was backstage at the Met Opera as an understudy in a production of *Così Fan Tutte* (an equally unlikely setting for me), waiting to hear if I'd go on that night or not, when the news announced New York's pandemic shelter-in-place order. The grief of missing our closing night performance was replaced by every other grief. My apartment contained my entire life and I moved inside my pocket-size portion of anxiety, crossing off each and every canceled gig as it passed, each out-of-town engagement, each festival, until there were none. For the first time in the nine years I had been performing and hosting burlesque, I had nothing on my calendar. My costume closet had become a collection of oddities, curios that crowded my too-small room, colorful things that blurred into the background as I assumed my role as a fledgling psychotherapist, seeing clients remotely from my bed, eating in my bed, staying awake in my

bed through the sounds of ambulances and helicopters and fire-
works and stagnant silence.

That summer my roommates and I took pains to extract any
morsel of joy we could from our lives. A nesting pair of kestrels
started hunting from a weathervane across the street from our
apartment, which we reported on to one another during a seg-
ment of our dinner conversations we named "Bird News." We
recreated a second-class lunch meal that was served aboard the
Titanic and dressed up to eat it in our living room. We joined a
CSA and wrote a weekly communal menu based on the e-mailed
newsletter that announced what ingredients would be in the farm
share. That's also how I saw an ad that the farm was looking for
an emcee for the Long Island Garlic Festival, a four-day gig held
over two weekends. I applied, desperate for any semblance of a
performing life, and after convincing the staff I could work a mic
without using profanity, I got the job. What's up, motherfuckers.

My friends and I drove to Long Island, past a church with
cardboard graves emblazoned with the names of George Floyd,
Ahmaud Arbery, Breonna Taylor, past their next-door neigh-
bors with hand-painted Trump signs. We pulled into the farm
lot, which was achingly green in that end-of-summer way. The
farmer met me by the car, already frantic, and she walked me to
the tent I'd be working in all weekend.

When I emcee burlesque, I am only responsible for turning
out a look, working the mic, running the raffle, and keeping the
show running on time. On the farm, I had a body that could do
work, so I was put to task. My first job was to set up the event
tent, dragging wooden farm tables out to my staging area, digging up rocks to keep plastic tarps from blowing away in the

wind, hooking up the PA system, placing chairs, carting supplies back and forth across the farm to my station, and collecting
donated raffle items from all of the vendors as they set up their
booths. I was in charge of the setup, execution, and cleanup for
three events a day: a talk by a local farmer about how to grow
garlic, a youth cooking competition on butane camping stoves,
and a raw-garlic-eating contest. Running events start to finish is
something I had exhaustingly practiced at the sex shop during
workshops, usually with a staff of two. The sex shop closed at 7
p.m. on Sundays and the workshops started at 7:30, so within a
half hour the rickety wooden display islands would need to be
moved or cleared, sixty chairs set out, all of the paper materials
collated and distributed, condoms and bananas and pens placed
on chairs, champagne poured, display toys and dildos brought to
the front, guest list compiled, all before the doors opened. Then
I'd teach the workshop for two hours, and we'd undo all our
work, put chairs back, wash the dildos, peel spit-slicked condoms
and banana bits off the chairs and floor, replace the islands, take
out the trash and recycling . . . you get it. I was out of practice and
out of my element on the farm, but I knew the drill.

Over the walkie-talkie hooked into my jeans, the farmer told
me to ask anyone for a hand with anything I needed. But everyone around me was busting their ass, dragging their own carts,
making sales, restocking gourds, tapping kegs. Farm workers
are a different sort of folk, imbued with the actual indefatigable industriousness that Americans in general often incorrectly
assign to themselves. I've never seen so many people work so
hard: thin older white women with wispy silver buns and over-
size sweatshirts, brewery apprentices from Ghana and Nigeria,

Mexican laborers in the kitchen, the farmstands, the fields. My friends Tim and Laura were kind enough to join me in the tent and separate heads of garlic, stacking paper cups of five cloves with frantic speed while I tested the mic and welcomed arrivals to the festival, who were starting to filter in and mill about.

After six months of being off the mic, hearing my own voice amplified and projected from the PA bathed me in narcissistic comfort.

"Gooooood morning, garlic aficionados! Welcome to the Long Island Garlic Festival! My name is Fancy Feast, and I will be your femme-cee today over here in the event tent. As you grab garlic garlands and gobble goodies from our fabulous local vendors, make sure to stop over and say hi, because we have events all day and prizes to give away!"

Ugh. *Yes.*

After spending so many months confined to my room, the expansive pastures of the farm felt alien. I had not been around that many people since the Met, save for protests, which I attended with prickling anxiety and rage, and which felt anything but safe. At the farm, groups of friends in masks strolled past cooking demonstrations and piles of late-summer vegetables. Families with babies in strollers shared sandwiches at picnic tables. It was as if I'd been bumped into an adjacent string of existence, one with pleasure, fresh air, and other people. I was exhilarated to make acquaintances, after months of speaking only to my closest loved ones and to my clients. In my journeys from the event tent to the walk-in refrigerator and kitchen and back, vendors called out hellos and joked with me about getting my steps in for the day. A blonde woman who'd worked the festival before helped me organize my station and dropped offhand complaints about her ex into our conversation (he does his best, he's just been through a lot and isn't good to be around), and I nodded and *uh-huh*ed with my hands on my hips like we hadn't all just been traumatized by living cheek to cheek with death and collapse. To my thrill and delight, the farmer's teenage son decided that I was old and out of touch and therefore not interested in his business, and he flirted with a teen girl working at the farm store for the season as he set up extension cords. The winners of the first day's cooking competition were a team of two, a queer couple that called themselves the Garlic Gaze/Gays, and they hugged as I handed them their prize, a wicker basket of soaps and canned goods and garlic from the farm. A returning champion of the garlic-eating contest came back to defend his title and won handily, then stayed near the event tent for fragrant chit-chat. I was getting the *Meet Me in St. Louis* treatment. The fair is in town, there's prizes to be won, and people are falling in love.

My friends had left me a sandwich to eat, and by the time I was able to take a break at the end of the last event, the swift organic processes of life on the farm had claimed it. It was roiling with ants, so I tossed it and gulped water and ate some beef jerky I'd packed, stealing a moment of privacy in the musty antechamber of a turnip shed.

After the day's exertions, the farmer drove me to her house, where she'd made up a guest room for me. We rolled into the gravel driveway, where we were greeted by the dramatic flop-over of Caramel, a wiry orange and white farm cat with a bubble-gum-pink nose who inspected me effusively and climbed into my arms for affection. I dragged my body to the backyard. Caramel kneaded claw holes into my neck as I watched the sun set over the fields in a bucolic watercolor. The evening breeze vented fresh, grassy air. Across the field, a single sheep eyed me with suspicion. The farmer's husband built a bonfire. We ate hot dogs and talked about travel, and that night I slept for nine full dreamless hours, my first solid sleep since the pandemic began, snuffed out of the conscious world by overwhelming and honest labor.

The next morning, the maskless vendor selling sheets, pillow-case sets, and $5 MAGA hats approached me as I set up the event tent. He flashed an inscrutable smile.

"Thanks to you I gave away a sheet set to a lesbian couple in that gift basket." My lungs vacuum-sealed shut.

"Yes," I said. "They won the competition."

"They looked pretty . . . lovey-dovey."

"They must have been happy they won. They made a great pasta dish."

"Well. There's a first time for everything. I have a joke about lesbians but I didn't tell it to them. They didn't seem like the type that could take a joke. I'm a comedian. I mostly do stand-up for kids. But I have some other material as well. Remind me to tell you the lesbian joke. I think you'll like it." He waved and walked off. My toes tightened inside my wool socks, and I tried to catch my breath.

I was caught off guard again that day during the cooking competition, for which I was obliged to remain on the mic for forty-five minutes. Do you have forty-five minutes of clean, entertaining prewritten material? I sure didn't, so I was desperate for crowd work. In the midst of a rousing garlic-themed trivia interlude, I heard the welcome sound of a heckler (anything to eat up some time!) and looked up to see a cluster of men in MAGA shirts and hats. I summoned my professionalism, or my cowardice, and the heckler and I bantered about garlic only. At the end of the competition, after the winner was crowned and I'd gathered the dirty dishes and leftover food and ingredients, the MAGA guys congratulated me on my set and said they hoped I'd come back the following year.

As I packed up at the end of my workday, a nondescript white guy sat in the shade of the event tent on the phone.

"Yeah—I bet she's a big fan of Nancy Pelosi. Ha! That's what I told her. So scared of the virus. The Jews are the high-risk ones for COVID anyway—they're not healthy people. It's the genetics, and they're overweight, especially the women. I know! I know! She's a moron."

My skin flushed red with rage, reacting to the threat, and I left my things in the shed as I fled the tent in haste. I sat in the recreation area and took deep breaths while a band of graying hippies played a cover of "Teenage Wedding." A tipsy sun-roasted Long Island woman in a sweater with cut-out shoulders step-touched along to the music on the patio with a beer in her hand and her mask under her chin, and I watched her until it was safe to get my bag and head to the bus.

The following weekend was smoother, less frantic. A man with a thick Eastern European accent and coarse black hair on every inch of his body won the garlic-eating competition, consuming forty-five raw cloves of garlic, skin on, in two minutes, shattering all previous records in festival history. I spotted the farmer's teenage son giving the girl a piggyback ride, which felt like a Very Big Deal. I developed a deep fondness for one of the farmhands because I could see her thinking up sarcastic remarks that her restraint and decorum wouldn't permit her to share, and she and I snuck glances and smirks at each other throughout the day. Our parting at the end of the festival caught me with unexpected grief.

Feedback on my work filtered from guests through to the farm staff, and I accepted the invitation to return the following year with gratitude for having something on my calendar. After the festival, the farmer invited me to go to the beach with her. The summer was over, and the beach was cold, even with a sweater. But being chilly was my city mouse nonsense. She threw off her sweatshirt and dove into the water, swimming toward the horizon with accelerating speed. I watched from the pebbled shore. Streaky clouds were strung across the sky and blew past a dimming pink sun. The day felt precious. I was already anticipating the ache of a hard winter. I tried to keep the feeling of the wind in my body and the sound of the waves in my brain; they washed out ceaselessly. I was, I am, trying to grasp onto things that are falling away from me, some small things and some very big.

Darlinda Just Darlinda was in the area that day visiting a friend's vineyard. She picked me up in her van to drive back into the city; she was dressed in layers of vivid, rainbow-hued clothing, wearing a mask printed with an illustration of herself dancing in the nude. When she laughed, it jiggled her likeness's ass. She stood out against the landscape like an exotic bird, and seeing her made me feel at home.

In Darlinda's burlesque classes, she talks about the Latin root of the word *entertain*—*tenere*, to hold. When stage work is done right, the audience will feel held by the performer: in their thrall, sure, but also held in a place of comfort. The emcee is the master of ceremonies, and the performance of mastery is what allows everyone else to relax into their roles. Skilled emcees can survive terrifying or anxiety-inducing performances without ever communicating as much to the audience. There's a kind of mirroring at play in a theater, the kind we learn to do with our caregivers when we are babies, to match the state they project to us for survival. So, the last thing an emcee wants is to have anyone in the crowd worry for or about them. It's hard to get back to a place of holding after that. Sometimes I wish I were less trained in assuring the comfort of the people around me. It's a hardwired skill of womanhood, of show business, and it has come in handy, especially because I've made the commitment to work everywhere I can, not only for the rooms that feel most comfortable. I'm interested in the frontier. I can only know the shape of something by exploring all of its contours, and I want to see what I can get out of being in places that weren't made for me.

Besides, if I only worked in rooms where I could guarantee that the producer, the venue, and all of the performers were aboveboard in their personal convictions and their politics, I would do maybe a gig a month. There's a hypocrisy you have to learn to anticipate when political art collides with commerce.

If you want to work, you will get comfortable accepting money from people with shitty beliefs or unethical practices. People like to lift up what I do as feminist, but there are nights when I can't believe that's true. It doesn't feel revolutionary when a venue owner who's probably racist and yells at his wife hands me a check. It does, however, feel like work, work that has required unexpected champions and imperfect allies to keep me employed and employable. My job is not an empowerment fairy tale or pure liberated artistic expression, untouched and unsullied by capitalism's grubby fingers. Playing up the girl power of burlesque is, in a way, a business decision—telling a story that people want to hear, a story that gets rewarded. I figure that capitalism requires me to experience some fundamental level of exploitation, so I may as well be an active participant in my own sausage-making. If that sounds gross, it is. But I'm here, taking off my clothes in the real world, not the imagined one. All money is dirty money, and I'd rather make it than not.

Burlesque is a permission slip, and permission slips are conditional and temporary, revoked after the trip is over. Being a performer means I keep being invited to places I wouldn't be welcome in otherwise. I have a role to work within, and without it, I would be less safe and less happy, so within it, I make do. That's the ceremony: being uncomfortable and not letting it show. I am on a tightrope. I keep making friends. I keep making money. The money is dirty. I play my part. I am inclusive and warm, a container, an entertainer. I regulate my breathing. I love my job. I cash my check. I project onto and receive the projections of others. I keep expecting enemies. I wish I could let go of that. I keep holding on.

Call Girl

. . . .

The voice on the other end of the phone asked if I would role-play an orgy at a law firm. I squeezed my eyes shut and said yes. Coarse blue industrial carpeting came into view, a wooden conference table laden with platters of meats and sweating cheeses impaled on festive toothpicks. I saw a room that was brighter than it should have been for a sensual atmosphere because of the fluorescents, which were required to remain on as part of the building's fire code. And I saw the partners of the firm, men and women in untailored suits sitting on stacks of briefs, leaning forward over keyboards, spreading their legs in swiveling office chairs. The voice on the other end of the phone did most of the talking while I added set dressing, details like the sound of a brown leather belt unbuckling, glances between two married partners whose kids had played together at the company picnic, the squeak of sweating, naked bodies pressed against the gurgling water cooler. The man the voice belonged to came after an hour. He broke the silence of the afterglow.

"This is your first day?"

"Yes, I'm absolutely brand new! Congratulations on being my very first."

"Well, let me give you some advice, since you're new. If you have a guy who calls you and asks you to repeat a phrase in Latin, don't do it. One of the girls on here had that happen to her, and she looked it up, and it was a phrase that opens a portal to hell."

I paused, watching my cat dream as she slept on my sweater. "Oh, that sounds *bad*. I wouldn't want to do that."

I worked a phone sex line during the first winter of the COVID-19 pandemic. December 2020 was desolate, and I had grown tired of learning embroidery, making mosaics, and baking cinnamon rolls. I hadn't been kissed in a year. More than that, no one had tucked cash into my stockings in nine months. No audience. No applause. I felt declawed, rendered in two dimensional planes. Nobody needed Fancy to exist. Nobody needed a good-time girl with overdrawn lips who could work a crowd. There were no crowds. The only version of myself that anyone asked for was the therapist, the me that interpreted and validated and made space for the depression and terror of a most awful winter. My therapist self was the most recent piece of me and therefore the least lived-in. I dragged her out every day in front of the computer for teletherapy, a stuffed puppet who nodded sagely, who made herself not-too-big, whom no one else would have to care for or worry about. Being a therapist had become the primary function of my life, and I was grateful to have even that. My clients continued to show up and work on themselves, taking our virtual sessions sitting in their dry bathtubs or in coat closets for lack of privacy in studio apartments, or from city sidewalks while ambulances screamed past. They apologized for the noise, as if it was something they had done. During the worst weeks, when it felt like death was pressing into the city like smog, the video-conferencing service would automatically mute both my and my clients' microphones because the sirens on both ends were too loud for the session to continue. And so we sat with our hands in our laps, looking at one another and waiting for it to pass.

I was lucky to be employed, but I was a mess. Being a therapist during an ongoing mental health crisis is challenging even when it's just one client who is going through it. Of course, all of my clients were falling apart, and so was I. I had not slept a full night since March. The only way I could guarantee privacy and confidentiality for my clients was to work from my bedroom, which meant working from my bed. I lit scented candles during the day and kept overhead lights off in the evening to differentiate my working hours from my resting hours, but that wasn't enough to guarantee an evening of slumber. Over the summer, one of my social work colleagues biked over after a protest to drop off a friendly blue container of sleeping pills, which I used to knock myself out when I had a long day ahead. I delayed existential dread by sprinkling coffee grounds in the soil of my verdant tomato plant, given to me by someone with an overly successful garden who posted it in a Buy Nothing Facebook group and passed up the other respondents because she had seen my show and was a fan. I moisturized my hands with homemade lotion. I stretched and did squats on my roof with a backpack full of cans of beans and thought about screaming. I marched. I passed out water bottles to protesters. I looked at anything green that was living. I told my jaw to relax but it stayed screwed tight. In the fall, my days mellowed into smeary doldrums, the Jane Austen tempo of conversation, long walks in a garden, bending over my embroidery until bedtime. I couldn't think about mortality anymore. I couldn't conjure wisdom and spend all day thinking about depression, illness, collapse. I needed to be jolted out of my own head, and I missed the life-giving filth that had always been a part of my adulthood. I was sick of my own thoughts. It didn't matter what sort of input I received as long as it wasn't of my own creation. So I opened a phone sex profile, to give texture to the bleak and the dark.

I didn't think people still had phone sex. It felt like the kind of thing people did in the nineties. I imagined a commercial on late-night insomnia television showing a babe in a tight dress with feathered hair and red nails, lonely on the other end of the line, waiting for a call. It was all greased lenses in my fantasy, but the reality was more banal. Niteflirt, a phone sex service, aligns with my nineties fantasy by having a user interface they haven't touched since Y2K. I was comforted by the prompts, which asked me to add my own HTML to format my profile, like I was back on LiveJournal and the internet was still wild and good. I was stepping out of the shower when I got my first call, and I skidded to my room on wet feet. My stomach lurched. What was I getting myself into? I lay face down on my bed with the towel below me and stepped into a law firm orgy. By the time he hung up, I had $137 in my account and the tools I needed to avoid a hellmouth.

My brain, working alone, could not have conjured any of that. What a delight.

When my roommates left the apartment for small, facsimile Christmases, I was alone for the first time in a year, and on Christmas Eve I reorganized my rhinestones while listening to podcasts and waiting for callers. One man called me from his bathroom, where he masturbated frantically, tinny holiday music and peoples' voices leaking through the locked door. Another caller, a sexually prolific martial arts instructor, told me stories of his escapades with strangers all over the world. Between calls, I shoveled chicken fried rice into my mouth and sang Connie Francis songs in my empty apartment. The steady stream of intimate novelty offered me the kind of nosy joy that I remembered from sitting on the subway and craning my neck to read a stranger's book: soft, parasocial company.

At 1 a.m. on a silent Friday night in January, I picked up the phone to find a new caller, young and British, blackout drunk.

"You fucking bitch. You've got me tied to your bed. Undo me." Not my favorite, to start a scene without negotiating first.

"Give me one good reason to untie you."

"Because I'll fucking kill you if you don't."

"You'll kill me if I do, so I guess I won't. Looks like you're stuck until I'm done with you."

He chortled. "Cheeky thing, are you? You nasty fuck—oh shit, I'm fucking cold."

"You're what?"

"I'm cold. I have a T-shirt on and I'm in the fucking garden."

"You should go inside. I don't want you to get hypothermia."

"I should, shouldn't I. You're not a bitch, are you, bitch? Are you—are you being good? Safe?"

"Yes, I'm inside and I'm safe."

"Good, good, because I have lost a lot this year and I'm taking care of my parents. Are your parents okay? Are they healthy?"

"They are. They're safe and healthy."

"Good, good. I'm sleepy."

"You should go to bed then. Can you go inside and go to bed?"

"Don't tell me what to do, you cunt."

"I'm the cunt who has you tied to my bed and I'm ordering you to go inside or at least put a sweater on."

"Right, well. I hope you have a good night."

"You, too."

One man sent me a $20 tip out of the blue and asked if I would consider doing fembot roleplay with him. Nothing could have appealed to me more. I could be paid to be a brainless thing, a respite from the intense emotional and interpersonal demands that had ground me down into a nub. I had a million questions for him: Did I pass the Turing test? What was my voice like? Would I malfunction, and if so, how? Did I know I was a robot? If so, how did I feel about it? Fetishes are never just the thing, I've found. Knowing a dude is into robot women is like knowing someone likes food. It's simply not enough information. There are obedient robots; lifelike robots; malfunctioning robots; robots that are programmed to say yes, programmed to say no; robots that don't know they aren't human. So I kept asking, he kept responding, and I honed my character into his perfect cyborg companion. He sent me more money for my enthusiasm and my attention to detail, and that was how I began spending large swaths of my day in robotland, inert and inanimate. For fun, I looked at myself in the mirror and went dead-eyed while I talked to him, allowing my gaze to follow a second after my head turned, like I was on a mechanical delay, just like he said. No need to be a human being ever again. Not when being a robot meant more profit and less pain.

My callers needed me to be exactly who or what they pictured. For many of them, a cam girl adds too much information with her body, with the details of her room, for the perfect projective fantasy to take place. The men who called me were looking for something both blank and elaborate, the perfect girl who could embellish their wishful thinking with enough texture to make it feel real, but not so much that the girl on the other end of the phone might wade into view. So I whispered behind smokescreens, the perfect mistress for one caller, the perfect little brat for the next. One of my callers had a fantasy scenario so elaborate, I kept multiple Google Docs with lists of my notes, size charts from men's millinery companies, and sound effect databases so I could meet all of his needs. My customers called me back. One caller wanted to pick me up from a farmers market and share a beer on my porch, then fuck me against my kitchen island while I put away my produce. He described how he would spank me after he told me not to refrigerate the tomatoes. After he came, we went back to the farmers market in our minds, both fantasizing about walking around among people and not feeling afraid of plague. I built up a roster of regulars. I exceeded my monthly income goal, and then did it again, and again.

I blocked some nasty callers: men who were furious that I wouldn't use the N-word for them, men who needled me to violate the site's terms of service, men fucked up on drugs. My least favorite guy was a loyal devotee of mine for many months. He fantasized about a scenario where he and I transformed into cartoonish caricatures of one another. Over time, he would eat more and gain weight so that his body became plump and more feminine, and I would commit to a grueling gym routine until I was a hulking mass of muscle and toxic masculinity. In our play, he claimed to have lost control of himself and he cast me as his bully, relentlessly teasing him for his womanhood and his weight. "Why are you doing this to me?" he asked, and I had no answer to offer. I despised how he urged me to say cruel things to him as he imagined inhabiting a body like mine. Once he sent me a photo of himself in a horrific acrylic wig and cheaply made lingerie, with lipstick applied to his face as if by shot put. "Getting closer to becoming you every day," he said, and rage flowed into my veins. I could not maintain my sanity being basted by his shame. His money wasn't worth it. I got rid of him.

Maybe I was cracking. One night, I expended a precious REM cycle dreaming about breaking quarantine protocols and hopping onto an empty red-eye train that spit me out at the mouth of Lake Michigan. I sat alone in the dim dawn with my feet dangling off a pier, watching my reflection emerge in the weak light. My phone rang. On the other end of the line, a man with a low, husky voice said hello with the breath pattern of someone already masturbating.

"C'mon," he said. "Tell me."

"When you look down into the water, all you can see is blue," I said. "It's cool, but not cold, and it feels fresh. From where I am sitting, the water reaches my ankles comfortably, and there is a gentle wave that laps at my skin when I'm not moving. It's very still here, and I'm all alone. It's, mmn, serene. I'm in a serene place."

He masturbated while I described the water until I woke up.

The next night, I was on with one of my regulars, a sturdy Montana man with bottomless stamina and a voice that reminded me of oak trees. As he approached his next orgasm, his voice shot out at me, urgent.

"SAY IT."

"Say what?"

"I love you."

"I love you, Michael."

"Again."

"I love you, Michael."

"God, I love you."

He didn't. The men were not well. No matter how much I tried to escape reality, it caught up with fantasy at every turn. I drew on some of my clinical skills, which accelerated the mounting feeling of burnout. My callers were so clearly going through it, and they needed to believe in me, in my attraction to them, in my fondness for them, in the mutual nature of our asymmetric relationship. I did my best work with the men who bought into that story of us. They called most often, and we got to know each other, or some version of each other. We grew warm and familiar. I began to take more calls from them that were completely nonsexual, just conversation and company. There was something dangerous about this kind of call, even if it was my favorite. When callers caught feelings for me, they would begin to question the financial nature of our relationship, even though that was the mutual agreement underlying our interactions from the get-go. If I really liked them, why were they still paying for access to me? This question tortured them until they brought it up with me, or until they blocked me, unable to cope. I could not tell them that for me, my fond feelings toward my favorite callers had nothing to do with feelings of romance or attraction. My feelings meant having a good night at work and little else. How could anyone be duped into believing this was anything but fantasy?

After a few months, my phone sex earnings outstripped my monthly therapist wages. My callers had started to blur in my mind. I wrote down as many names as I could remember so I wouldn't be caught reintroducing myself to someone I had already had a passionate tryst with. Which Dave is this—Daddy Dave, Dave from Canada who's into edging, or the Dave that wants me to turn into a frog? Moreover, which me am I? I had put Fancy away but created another persona, and she was hard to turn off. When friends called to check in on me, I forgot that I wasn't getting paid by the minute to speak to them. I stopped volunteering information about myself first and tried to take cues from my loved ones about what they wanted to talk about, just like I did with my callers. Once again, I found myself shrinking. There was no point in wanting—wanting to be outside or with my family or friends—so how could I become the most devoid person possible, smooth edges only?

No need to think about myself or worry about my life. A new caller was on the line. He sputtered a little during his introduction and asked me how my day was going. Noah's buoyant, brainy voice immediately put me at ease.

"Do I launch into it?" he asked. "I feel like a fucking weirdo for just leaping into telling you about my fetish. I should at least buy you a drink first."

"You're very sweet, but this is the phone sex line," I said. "If this were a work conference call, that would be one thing."

He was a cuckold, he told me, which for him meant that his ideal relationship was asymmetrical. His girlfriend could and should feel free to go out and pursue other men, and he would remain loyal to her and only her. He would understand his place within the relationship as inherently subordinate, fundamentally not enough; he twisted on the skewer of his not-enoughness, the core component of his sexuality.

"I don't want to be one of those useless cuck guys though, who are just like a drag to be around because they are too much of a mess. I need to be in good enough working order to be fun for someone to fuck with."

It wasn't fun for him unless it hurt, unless the stakes were real, unless his head was being played with somehow. I told him about my Celine Dion torture scene* and he told me about his lingering sexual response to *Blade Runner* forged under similar circumstances. The conversation took a detour and we compared

---

* Turns out you can train someone to respond sexually to a Celine Dion song if you play it enough times under sexually stimulating circumstances. Long story. Buy me lunch and I'll tell you.

notes about our favorite sci-fi short stories. The chemistry was fast and easy. I found myself wondering what he looked like. He was witty, self-effacing. I guessed his age and that he had had a crush on a teacher in high school, including the year and the subject (senior, English). I propped myself up in bed on my elbows, feet in the air like a schoolgirl, and we made each other laugh until his money ran out. He wrote to me later to say thank you for putting him at ease.

He bought a collection of my photos and left me a positive review. He sent me a couple of pictures of himself, tall and lanky, dusted with Jew-y body hair, looking straight at the camera with stormy eyes. I liked how he positioned his body, coquettish, a little feminine, objectifying himself for the viewer. I answered right away the next time I saw him call. We picked up where we'd left off, then went deeper. We talked about how I would tease him, grazing his body but not touching him outright, how I would make him beg for me. He asked for my permission to touch himself, and I said no. I told him that he would only ever see me in comfy cotton panties because he didn't deserve to see me in sexy lingerie. I told him to imagine being on his knees, his face an inch away from my pussy, not permitted to touch or taste me. He asked to touch himself again, and I said no. He told me he felt crazy, or drunk, that he wanted me so bad it hurt. I kept whispering in his ear about the other men whose cocks I would happily fuck or suck but how this was the only thing he would ever get from me. His breathing changed, and I realized he was crying.

"When I talk to you, I feel like I'm going to die," he said.

"Okay," I hissed, "so die."

I granted him permission to touch himself, and he came shortly thereafter in whimpers and heaving gasps. He got quiet, and I wondered if he felt alone, gripped by a postorgasmic endorphin drop.

"Now I'm going to the kitchen and getting you a glass of water," I murmured into the phone.

"No, you're not," he said. "Getting water is my move. I'm getting you water."

"We are both getting each other a glass of water," I replied, "which is inefficient but, nevertheless. And then I pull you into me, back down into the bed, so that even though you are so much taller than me, you are still the little spoon. And I'm drawing you in, holding your hips so that we are resting against each other."

"That sounds nice."

"And I'm running my fingers through your hair and over your scalp, tracing your temples, and I'm kissing your shoulder blade and telling you how proud I am of you, of what you did tonight, of how it made me feel."

"I've never had phone sex where there was aftercare. Why are you being so nice to me?"

"Because I am a responsible top!" I sighed. ". . . Because I like you."

"I like you, too." I pressed my ear to the phone to hear him breathe.

I made my own hours, so I found myself logging in around the times of day I figured he would be getting off work. He tipped me generously and asked me to send him a song he could listen to when he was thinking of me. I picked Perfume Genius's "Queen," and he wrote the next day to say he was looking at my photos and listening to it on repeat. Images started flooding my mind, me burying my head into his soft, flimsy T-shirt, waking up under a sheet with him, sitting on his lap and making out in a big comfy armchair. I thought about getting brunch with him, meeting his friends, staying up late watching *Mystery Science Theater 3000*.

Shame shot through my bones. *Are you falling for a client, you fucking amateur?* This kind of thing isn't supposed to happen. I stopped enjoying my other calls, even my loveliest regulars. I was the powerful one, the domme, the girl in charge, but I had no way to call him, so I sat by the phone and waited, impotent. If I lowered my rate, I wondered, would he call more? I was weak, a cliché, and it was getting worse.

"You're really good at your job," he said to me one day. "I feel like I understand every fucking idiot guy who falls for the stripper or whatever. I'm one of them. A complete simp for you."

"I am aware that everything I say is going to sound like a line because it's so unoriginal, but I actually feel different about you than I do about any of the other people who call me. I think we have a connection. And you don't have to believe me that I am not bullshitting you. But if it feels real, I mean, it's because it is. Actually, uh . . . never mind."

"What? You have to tell me!"

"No, it's a bad question."

"I don't know. You've heard me come and cry. You can ask me."

"Where do you live?"

"Baltimore."

"Oh."

"Where do you live?"

"New York."

"Oh."

"That's a pretty quick train ride away."

"I know."

Could this be the worst possible way to meet someone? Had I done it? Had I landed the ugliest meet-cute of all? *You met on a train? That's so romantic! Oh, high school sweethearts—how charming! Us? Noah and I met because he was my phone cuck. You know, he paid to jerk off with me on the phone? While I talked about fucking other men! It's a funny story really: we were both losing our minds during the pandemic winter and falling apart emotionally, and after a few weeks of calling him worthless and pathetic I just kind of . . . knew! You know that feeling? When every day is a kind of ego death and you sense yourself slipping into the abyss, but then you meet someone and it just clicks?*

Noah could spin himself out onto a frantic existential limb with no prompting whatsoever, and I joked that he didn't even need me to be there to humiliate him on our calls. I could set my phone down and paint my nails while he self-destructed on autopilot. He doubted himself. The intensity of his feelings frightened him. His obsession with me dislodged clumps of shame that neither of us knew what to do with. His self-loathing welcomed my cruelty, and he only ever questioned what he called my kindness, expressions of my affection and regard. I love a self-loather. I was falling for him, so I had more softness and sweetness to give him, and that enlarged his distrust. He craved my softness and pushed it away. I imagined taking care of him while he was sick, making him soup and tea. I thought about holding his head in my hands and kissing his forehead while I spoke violence into his eager ears.

"If we met—" I started one morning, staring out the window, watching snowflakes loop-de-loop in the milky sky.

"Yeah?"

"If we met, we would be moving out of a fantasy place and into a reality place."

"Yes, necessarily we would."

"I'm protective of your fantasy of me. You deserve it, and I enjoy what you're projecting onto me. I wouldn't want you to lose that, because if we met there'd be no way to get back there."

"I know, but I also think you're discounting how much reality appeals to me. I want the kind of mundane, everyday details of a person. Like, what you might smell like after a long day, when you're not done up or fresh. I don't know. I just want that. It's so intimate. Am I gross? God, I'm gross."

"You're not gross. I get it. Would it be worth the trade-off?"

"I don't know. I think so. Would I pay you?"

"I don't know. It's a lot to think about. The money creates a boundary, and maybe that's a good thing. But I don't know. Let's just keep getting to know each other."

Noah and I talked about therapy. He was working on healing from a porn addiction. The phone sex site felt like a better and more connected way to get off, and his therapist knew about it and was supportive. But he was getting conflicted. He could feel himself being drawn into the site, into me, in ways that didn't feel healthy to him. He wasn't calling me as often, but he told me he was thinking about me every day. I worried about the fact that he and I were operating on different schedules. He was busy with work, and Saturday was his day off. Saturdays were my day off, too, but despite myself, I logged in and took calls hoping he would be on, while my roommates made brunch on the other side of my bedroom door, while I waited for Tiger to come over to lift weights with me in the living room. To be wanted and then to be wanted less, pursued less, was devastating. I wanted to chase the high but all I could do was log in and wait for him to show. Eventually, he did.

"So is this site antithetical to your healing?" I asked him in a moment of postorgasm sobriety.

"I don't know. Yes. No. It might be. I wasn't expecting to feel this way about you."

"Yeah, me neither. It's a bit of a mindfuck. I'm going to be going home to DC after my parents get vaccinated. Just something to think about."

My vulnerability made me uneasy. Pharoah hardened her heart. The next time he called, I laughed at him and mocked him until he came, a crueler sadomasochistic experience than usual, and I heard the immediate shame spiral overwhelm him when our play was done. I crumbled inside and flooded the reservoir with apologies.

"This thing we do, it's intimate. I'm okay, I promise. I just got thrown for a loop," he said.

"I'm so sorry. I thought I was doing what you wanted. I thought you wanted meaner."

"We can do a redo next time we talk."

"Yes please. I'm already looking forward to it. Jesus, I'm sorry."

"Stop apologizing. I'm fine. Really."

We couldn't align our schedules that week. He was tired, work had been taking it out of him, he told me. He said he missed me. One day, I wrote to him to see how he was doing, and I received an auto-response: *Your message could not be delivered.* I checked my wifi and hit return again. He had closed his account.

I lost my taste for all of my jobs and walked circles around the park near my house in the dismal first days of spring. Some of my regulars reached out to ask if I was okay, and whether I would be on any time soon, and I told them I was sick. I was an idiot after all, the kind of hooker-with-a-heart-of-gold stereotype that would enrage me in any other circumstance. Did I think I was going to find love on the phone sex site? Really? Did I think that a self-hating sex addict cuck was going to have his shit together enough to be, what, my boyfriend? How had I allowed myself to have any of these feelings?

I hated to lose him, and I hated to lose. I sent a message to his inactive profile's inbox, the last remaining lifeline to his closed account.

Tried sending you a chat and it got bounced, so
maybe I'm blocked or you cashed out your account or
something. If you did decide to leave for a bit or for
good, I'm sad I didn't get a chance to say a proper bye
or "bye for now." My hope is that your absence from the
site is part of a recovery process, or part of something
that feels good for you and your growth/development/
healing. I suspect but can't confirm that your feelings for
me brought some things to a crisis point or contributed
to confusion, and I am sorry if that's the case.

It's been an isolating, fucked up year and talking
to you has been a bright spot in it for me—and I
wish that could continue. I can see how any sense of
my true intentions or feelings for you can be hard to
trust because of this weird, mediated site, and by the
associated boundaries and my desire for self-protection.
So I'll leave it with this last bit, just in case.

I closed the message with my phone number. He texted me
the next day.

I'd hit the nail on the head, he said. The site was fucking with
him too much and he had to step away from it. I asked if he
still wanted to talk as people, and he said he would, and that he
would appreciate it if it didn't get sexual. So we talked about the
opposite of sex (podcasts) and the conversation meandered into
a discussion about ferrets and then he sent me a photo of himself
waiting at a stadium for his vaccine appointment. We both had
plans to clean our apartments on Saturday; what if we spoke on
the phone and kept each other company while we tidied up? He
said he'd love that, and he'd call.

What would you like to have happened next? What happened
instead?

Here's my $1.99-a-minute fantasy version, the better end-
ing than reality, the one I'd rather tell. Let's say he called me at
noon, a little harried because he had gotten off the phone with
his mother and it was a whole thing he didn't want to get into.

He asked me how I was, how I slept, and I told him I didn't sleep well anymore, but fine enough. I asked him what chores were on his list for the day, and he balked.

"Isn't the whole point that you are supposed to be distracting me from what I'm doing? Are you trying to get me to, like, be mindful and aware of my present state?"

"I would never doom you to that, Noah. We can folie à deux together in a bit. I'm just comparing notes."

"I have to do counters, surfaces really. My roommates do a kind of geological thing with how they leave shit in piles. You could take a core of it and study it in a lab."

"Damn, and here I thought we were going to stay away from dirty talk."

Whenever I did chores on a Saturday afternoon, I called him. He had started to reemerge socially and was excited not to talk to the same five people. Work was still work, but it was varied with enough other things to keep his spirits high. Spring broke open like ripe fruit. My parents got vaccinated, which meant I was going home to DC.

"On my way back, though—" I said.

"Yes."

"Yes."

After six days of hugging my parents and eating out of the fridge like a teenage ne'er-do-well, I hopped back on Amtrak and vibrated in the Quiet Car until the train pulled into Baltimore Penn Station. He spotted me first, standing on the corner of Charles Street, looking through him because I don't wear my glasses like I should. He looked panicked, and fidgeted as he walked toward me, but I broke into a smile and so did he, and then he held me in his long, slender arms. I wanted to crush him against me, but I fought it to play it cool. Cool-ish.

"Look who it is!"

"I can't believe it."

We had lunch at an airy café with a wall of bookshelves. I was too nervous to eat so I picked at a salad and a cold brew, and he self-consciously downed a sandwich and apologized twice for no reason. We agreed to put the horrible year in its grave. He was doing better, he said, not all the way, but progress, not perfection, right? We clinked glasses and toasted to a banner year in our mental health. He joked that we should get out our phones and talk to each other that way, like old times.

He paid for lunch despite my protestations to the contrary. He had another hour before he had somewhere to be, and did I want to take a walk? We found a nice enough area with trees lining the street.

"I think if I don't make the first move, it's not going to happen, is that right?"

He looked over at me, incredulous. "Of COURSE. Who do you think you're talking to?"

"Okay, so then I'm going to ask you to stop walking and lean down a little because I'm going to kiss you."

It wasn't my best work, clumsy in execution, but when I held the back of his neck I felt the warmth of his skin in the sunshine and it silenced my inner critic. His mouth was soft. He held one of my curls in his fingers and passed his nose over it.

"So that's what your hair smells like."

"Good?"

"My new favorite thing."

I stumbled a little on the edge of a brick in the sidewalk that had become dislodged by the overgrown roots of a flowering tree, and wrinkled my nose as I looked up at him.

"Uh, I'm still very hip and dominant. I just am not great at standing right now."

"I'm still very intimidated by you."

"Good, great."

He walked me back toward the station.

"I get booked in DC and Baltimore all the time," I said, "and whatever, I don't need a reason to come. If you want, I would like to come back."

"Yes, of course. I want that."

"This has been so strange and so nice."

"This whole thing. So strange and so nice."

I leaned him against the smooth stone facade of the train station and kissed him again. He responded with grasping hands, pulling me into a hard embrace.

"I don't want to go," I said, tugging on his shirt.

"I don't want you to go, either."

"Say goodbye."

"Goodbye."

"Goodbye."

He stood on the corner and watched me until I was out of sight. Back on the Quiet Car, my phone lit up.

I have a big fat crush on you and you know it.

•••

Phone sex calls end with a woman's stilted, computerized voice saying, "ONE MINUTE REMAINING," and this is about where in the fantasy of us that I imagine getting that warning. My mind reels forward, wanting to fill in so much else in our final sixty seconds: fucking in a tangle of limbs and sweat-soaked hair; takeout and movies and laughing until the air is sucked from my lungs; holding his knees while he has a panic attack on the floor of his bathroom; drinks with my best friends; thrift shopping; recovering from our first big fight, where he freaks out so much that he needs me to care for him, which I resent, but we agree to work on it; mornings in bed; pulling out photo albums with his mom and seeing Noah at eleven with his award-winning science project, already tall with stretched-taffy limbs; trying to get him to dance to a song he hates; telling him my secrets but making him look at the wall when I say them out loud so I don't lose my nerve; getting some groceries; cooking and cleaning; sleeping and waking; burying my face into his armpit; singing in the car on the only good leg of a disastrous road trip; looking for the—

In the Field

· ·

There is one bus that will take you to Rikers Island. It wormwends its way through the up-and-coming part of Long Island City; up the commercial thoroughfare of Astoria, which is dotted by coffee shops, wine stores, and Greek restaurants; and across the Rikers Island Bridge, which spans the East River. Nothing else connects the island to the rest of the city except the dirty river water that laps at both shores, and as the Q100 bus approaches its final stop, the dense New York traffic drops away on all sides, and even the babies on the crowded bus get quieter. Female passengers carry clear plastic purses on their laps that crinkle and squeak between their fingers. No one stares into each other's bags, even with all of the contents visible—cell phones, money, keys, prescription medication, baby bottles. The clear purses streamline the process of inspection by correctional staff, so you can tell who has been making these visits for long enough to bring one.

The instant the bus parks outside the bleak, boxy Benjamin Ward Visitor Center, the lawyers and social workers who visit

Rikers have a two-second grace period to leap out before correctional officers, or COs, step aboard shouting, drug-sniffing dogs in tow. Inside the port of entry, the folks in business attire get to wait inside a cordoned-off area while the loved ones of the incarcerated are lined up against a wall and searched for contraband items, already accused of something. It often breaks neatly across races; the white attorneys with their IDs out on one side, and Black and brown families getting patted down with their hands against the painted cinderblock wall on the other. When it was my turn to be called, I handed over my ID card and my Secure Pass, which allowed me the same privileges as legal counsel within court and jail facilities, and provided documentation for the clients I was going to meet.

You're not allowed to walk between the individual jail facilities that make up the Rikers complex. Instead, you have to board the little white bus operated by the Department of Corrections that tools around between the visitor center and the island's nine jails every twenty minutes. If you're in a rush, no you're not. You are at the mercy of the schedules of the COs, their whims, and their lunch breaks. On my first visit, the shuttle did not come at all. I paced back and forth in front of the bus stop for forty minutes and then took off on foot toward the facility, grasping my files to my chest and practicing my apology in case I got stopped by guards.

Outside of the jail, I shoved my purse into a locker. The only lock I had with me was the kind that needs a key to open it, not a combination lock, so I tucked the two metal keys on a flimsy split ring into my sports bra, which I wore under my frumpy, formless dress. The entrance to the facility was two sets of locked doors, and the CO at the front desk buzzed me in one set at a time. Inside the reception area, civilians awaiting their visitation times clustered around industrial plastic chairs and a solitary, half-empty vending machine. When I was called forward, I checked in with the CO at the desk, who told me he would let me know when they had produced "the body"—the slang term they use for the living, incarcerated person I was visiting.

Fifteen minutes later, the CO pointed me to behind the reception area, deeper inside the facility. I entered another set of double doors, the first of which opened with the heavy, metal scraping sound of a locked-down, secured entry, a sound I'd only ever heard before at a dog groomer, the sound of escape prevented. The guards controlling that set of doors peered down at me through smudged plexiglass from an elevated platform two feet above my eyeline and muttered something incomprehensible into a buzzy microphone.

"Do you know where you're going?"

I turned around to see a man in a suit with a handful of manila case files standing in the same vestibule.

"I don't."

"First time here? Okay, when we get in, you can follow me."

We stood together with shared impatience as the COs monitored the hallway to make sure it was completely clear before buzzing us in. The energy shifted abruptly on the other side of the doors. Although the hallway was free of other people, it echoed with voices, footfalls, the sounds of doors buzzing and metal slamming. The air changed, too, flattening into a musky, windless doldrum. I followed the lawyer in front of me, who cut through the static, barreling ahead toward another guard. The guard looked at me and said, "Counsel room?" I nodded, and he led me to a door behind him and ushered me inside.

The seventeen-year-old on the other side of the partition looked surprised to see me.

Because I'm a nightlife performer who has a day job in mental health, I spend a lot of time negotiating the coexistence of all my selves. The me who inventories nipple pasties when I pack for the Slipper Room or the me who makes notes in the margins of the set list for the orgy preshow has just as much of a right to exist as the me who provides therapy from my bed during a pandemic or the me who works a phone sex line or the me who teaches cancer patients about lube. I want to have and do it all, and not foreclose any of the versions of me that might be asked to step forward in a given situation. That means that I have learned to make peace with the idea that someone, somewhere, might very well see their social worker onstage stripping. Someone who might have bought lube from me years ago is now in my waiting room seeking therapy. My old college professor might DM me for my expertise on sex toys. It's not a perfect system, and it sets me up for boundary negotiations that most people will never face, but it's how I've built my life, and I am not ashamed of a single part of it. It does mean, however, that I get the bends when I move too quickly between selves, and it can be hard to explain to other people how all of these parts even fit together.

Becoming a social worker is not only a labor of love; it is a labor of labor. New York state requires that each graduate-level social work student complete at least nine hundred hours of an unpaid field internship, and most schools require at least twelve hundred. At $15 an hour (NYC minimum wage), each student generates $18,000 in unpaid wages over the course of two years, an amount of money that would cover the cost of in-state tuition. This is by no means where the injustice starts or ends in the provision of social services, but it is one more way that injustice and inequity are baked into the field.

The schools place students at sites where they learn on the job, working directly with clients and communities, or within think tanks and nonprofits on behalf of policy initiatives. The insistence that these be unpaid "opportunities" disproportionately disadvantages low-income social work students, who must deviate from the official school recommendation that, due to the workload, no one enrolled in the programs should expect to work an outside job. The guaranteed influx of free labor to these nonprofits and organizations (in fact, students pay tuition for their field placements, effectively giving the school money to work) helps keep starting salary ranges for social workers nice and low. There is, of course, the expectation that these students will perform gratitude for the chance to work for free in a field related to their interests—regardless of whether, in practice, it actually is. If the student intern does not like the focus of their placement, they will be told to broaden their horizons and challenge themself to explore an aspect of the field they never thought they might be interested in pursuing. That is how, after specifying on my application form that due to my history of surviving rape and sexual assault, I would work with anyone but violent men, I was assigned to be a court advocate for people involved in the criminal justice system.

My job was to meet with clients facing criminal charges, to interview them and construct a psychosocial life history, a life story for everything up until the day of the alleged crime. What was their childhood like? What were their dreams, their hobbies? What trauma had they endured? This life history would be submitted in the form of a pre-plea memorandum to humanize the client in the eyes of the judge, who without this information would decide the case based on a rap sheet, a mug shot, and the story provided by an overburdened public defender, who might have as many as one hundred other active cases at any given time. A busy lawyer can't do all of the work necessary to provide comprehensive, competent representation for their clients, so they call in an advocate. Clients with advocates often end up with more lenient plea deals, serving less time in jail or prison, and paying lower fines, or are given offers of ATI programs, which are alternatives to incarceration in the community.

I spent my first week of onboarding tagging along with seasoned court advocates and sitting on courtroom benches while their clients' cases were called before a judge. Everything I knew about court procedure prior to this came from that chief source of white-woman true-crime content: *Law & Order: SVU.* The year after my film school sexual assault, the summer before my senior year, I spent a month alone in South Slope, Brooklyn, subletting a one-bedroom apartment, whipping through the first ten seasons and eating a bundle of roasted beets with braised beet greens every day until I developed an allergy. I *Clockwork*

Orange-d myself on rape, root vegetables, and the sturdy build of Detective Elliot Stabler until I dreamed at night of my own dismemberment, the unearthing of my scattered bones illuminated by the traffic circle stoplights at Grand Army Plaza.

Brooklyn Criminal Court does not resemble the stately, wood-paneled courtrooms of SVU. The fluorescent-lit courtroom feels like a cross between a classroom and a bus depot. Most of one's day there is spent waiting, sitting on long wooden benches and biding time until your case is called. The attorneys sit in the first or second row, in front of the wooden partition that separates the court employees from the public. Social workers and nonprofit advocates gather as close as possible to the front so they can confer with the lawyers representing their shared client. Behind them, family members crowd the remaining benches, there to support their loved ones. If the client is incarcerated, their court appearance will offer the family a rare glimpse of them outside of jail visitation. If the client is out in the community, they will need to arrive on time or else risk missing their appearance, delaying the case, and possibly facing additional penalties. If the day's docket of cases is backed up, and it often is, morning cases will get punted to the afternoon, after the hour-long lunch break. You can spend your whole day waiting, which is fine for a social work student but less so for family members with kids who have taken off work.

There are no stirring monologues like the ones TV writers drop into the third-act denouement of *Law & Order* episodes, unless your case is going before a judge who is partial to moralistic diatribes, or one who wants to use the court's precious time to deliver a soliloquy about his most recent vacation. Otherwise, things are quiet and stilted. The announcement of the next case is read aloud, but most of the actual proceedings are nearly sotto voce, out of earshot to most of the pews. Defendants are produced, either from the pews or from a side door in the courtroom, behind which the incarcerated clients await their cases. White defendants are so rare that when one is produced, bored attorneys' heads snap up and they lean forward to rest their elbows on the wooden guardrail while the charges are read. From what I saw, it was white-collar crime, mostly: tax evasion, insider trading, or sex crimes. Usually, they were still out in the community and appeared from among the gathered audience; it was even less common to see a white person produced from the other side of the door in a jumpsuit and handcuffs. The first time I saw a white "body" being produced, I heard an attorney mutter, "Well, *he* must have really fucked up."

My supervisor described the organization we worked for as the place where social workers go when their idealism has died. When someone is ready to crucify their martyr complex and shelve their mug that proudly proclaims in fifteen different fonts that they are a "badass, no-nonsense miracle worker," they will turn once more unto the breach of the criminal justice system. At school, fellow students marveled that my placement sounded "so hard." It was easier to imagine providing care for the "most deserving," for children, battered women, victims, innocents. A classmate asked me if I investigated the alleged crimes to exonerate the wrongfully accused. I grew staunch, snapping at my classmates who needed my clients to be innocent to think of them as deserving of care.

At our weekly case assignment meeting, the advocates took turns reading through the current charges and any attorney notes for each prospective client. If anyone tutted or sighed in reaction to a particularly gruesome detail of the crime, like a prospective client who had hit his girlfriend with a piece of pipe, our director rapped on the conference table with her fist. "ALLEGEDLY! PLEASE, people! It is not our job to judge this man!" Every advocate had some preference for which cases they took. Some people preferred to work with the clients housed at Rosie's, the women's jail. Others preferred working with youth or took cases that could be resolved with a referral to substance use treatment programs. Some advocates chose their cases based on the borough where the case was being seen or the specific judge assigned to it. Mackenzie, the honey-voiced advocate with a Disney smile and tinctures in tiny brown bottles on her desk, always snagged the rape and incest cases. Eventually I learned that I had a particular affinity for working with gang-affiliated people, most of whom were victims of other crimes in their early adolescence, most of whom had a history of childhood trauma. Who wouldn't seek safety and belonging in those circumstances?

After a few weeks of shadowing others, I was assigned my first solo cases, and it was up to me to arrange to meet with my clients, some of whom were out on bail and some of whom were incarcerated. Since going to Rikers was such an ordeal, there was an option to schedule videoconference sessions in a musty confessional room in one of the borough courthouses. The court employee who scheduled Manhattan's videoconferences was a big fan of Broadway shows, my coworker Julia told me. Ask about the playbills on his desk, bat an eye, and you might get your pick of appointments in the next round. I pointed to the *Hamilton* playbill on the clerk's desk.

"How did you get tickets?" I asked.

"You just gotta keep refreshing the site," he said proudly, "and if you stay patient, something will show up."

From then on, I could call last minute, not needing to heed the twenty-four-hour advance notice required to schedule video-conferences, provided I kept up the small talk.

I sat at my desk, tapping out my notes from my day's videoconferences into a Word document, when my e-mail pinged. Zoe Ziegfeld, a performer friend, had forwarded me a request for a "body positive" role in a forthcoming opera at the Met. One of the sopranos for *Mefistofele* needed a body double to appear nude in a scene, and the Met was having a hard time finding larger-bodied women who would feel comfortable being naked onstage. They were desperate and I was usually naked, and isn't that how the best love stories begin? Surely, though social work school had said not to take on outside work, they would make an exception for the Met.

I skipped class to drop off my onboarding paperwork, entering the city-block-size compound from a side door across the street from Juilliard. The network of windowless, underground hallways of the Metropolitan Opera exude the circuitous madness of the Winchester Mystery House. It's easy to get lost and stay that way. Staircases stop and stall out one floor up. Some elevators go to some floors, but it's not clear which, why, or where they are. Doors are nondescript, lacking placards, and they'll lead you to another hallway or into a private dressing room, an industrial laundry, a cavernous kitchen, or, as I discovered when

I was looking for the human resources office, a stable with live, snuffling horses. The subterranean employee cafeteria is open on two ends, and to get around to the correct entrance one must dodge racks of chairs, upright bass cases, and set pieces in transit: filigreed gazebos, golden calves, a teacup ride on wheels. As union men and maestros alike sit at round Formica tables with bagels and coffee, chewing under fluorescent lights, the PA system (which in any other setting would be broadcasting Muzak) pipes in gorgeous, orchestrated live opera from the stage.

I needed to get my measurements taken by the garment team. The Met Opera costume shop is in the attic of the building, an airless, low-ceilinged workshop swollen with racks of regalia. Costumers buzz around the hive in aprons, with mouths full of straight pins, fussing over bolts of fabric and decapitated dress forms padded with white and taupe foam to conform to the Teutonic proportions of the singers. The walls are lined with shelves of plastic bins with labels like "Roman helmets and pauldrons - BOYS," "Capezio tights - S-XXL," and "Bohème Wigs." There are reams of every trim and finding imaginable. I had found my Eden.

An employee checked me in and whisked me away to what they called "the Champagne room" (the head costumer despises this moniker), a name given to the mirror-lined antechamber where they measure performers for fittings.

"I don't mean to be rude," I said, "but I am going to appear naked, so why would I be getting measured for a costume?"

The employee laughed. "In case they want you to get a robe, or privacy garments, or tights. Or who knows, if you get asked back to do another opera, then we'll have your measurements on file." She snapped a few reference photos and sent me back through the maze.

For several weeks, I started my days at a jail and ended them at the Met, careening from one bracket of the city to the other, from the threshold of greatest suffering and erasure to the highest echelon of money and culture. I held my tongue all day. The nondescript, sexless day drag I wore to court and jail concealed my body. I tied my hair back in a messy bun, hoping no one would cast their gaze upon me with the flinty stare of recognition. I was not as slick as I thought I was. One day my coworker pulled me into her office to ask if she had seen me stripping out of a bee costume at Coney Island, and I assented with my eyes fixed on the cup of pens on her desk.

"Your secret is safe with me," she said. "I pro-dommed my way through grad school. Domming taught me most of the skills I use in court. I get it."

My role at the Met was called a cover, which is a type of understudy. I would learn the path of the actor hired to portray the role, attend rehearsals, and be backstage at every show in case I was needed. I covered for my friend Cristina, an actress I used to sell sex toys with, who was hired as a body double for a soprano who didn't want to appear in her own nonsinging nude scene. I shadowed her before and during performances, watching her every move, seeing how she did her makeup, first for a scene where she was being boiled in a pot on a parade float, and then for one where she appeared nude in a tower. I brought chocolate-covered nuts and clementines to share. When the stage manager called places, Cristina headed down to the backstage wings for her entrance, and I did my social work homework at a lit makeup vanity and chatted with the other understudies as they transformed into angels and demons.

At my internship, I was assigned a sixteen-year-old client, pregnant at Rikers, facing first-degree assault charges. She and I spoke once, for thirty minutes total, over videoconference. On a Monday, I wrote to the judge requesting she be released into the community without posting bail and the very next day, she was out. I had scarcely done any work for this to happen; why did a letter from some white grad student make such a difference? The next day I attended a party in one of the Met's grand foyers, chatted with donors, ate canapes, and shook hands with millionaires. That night, I took the 2 train downtown, transferred to the Brooklyn-bound L train by walking through that rectal, block-long underpass, past a table laden with noxious incense for sale and a cheerful man singing bouncy Beatles covers. When I'd finally turned my key in my lock and wiped the makeup off my face, I slept in fits and woke up just in time to commute to East Harlem for school in the morning. To get to my internship the next day, I waded through hundreds of student protesters demonstrating in front of the courthouse, demanding an end to gun violence in schools. I pushed past their handmade signs to attend the sentencing of a client who had become gang-affiliated after being shot outside of his own home as a child. His family was too heartsick to go, so I was the only one aside from his attorney there for him. He and I stood before the judge on opposite sides of his counsel. He stared straight ahead, blank. When he turned and noticed me, he smiled, and so did I, then the judge handed down his five-year sentence. That night, when I returned home from work, my apartment felt impossibly large, my bed absurdly soft. I ate fresh figs with honey and yogurt in bed and felt sorry for myself, my head woozy, as if I'd been hiking in high altitude. In the span of a week, I had stared into the expanse of an empty food pantry with a hungry client and overheard blue-haired women in gowns complain about the declining quality of the catering's blini, and there I was, crying in my sheets with a bowl of good, fresh food between my knees. God bless America, I'm fucking dizzy. In God We Trust, get me off this ride. I had seen too much at once and had nowhere to allocate the feeling. Hurtling back and forth between the campsites of New York's class inequality every day was making me sick.

I began to wonder how many other people had been to both this jail and to this opera, a distance of five and a half miles as the crow flies. The opera staff, I reasoned, were more likely to have made that journey than the patrons, because the wealthy do not do such things. Maybe one of the security guards manning the front desk had gotten his start with a stint at Manhattan Detention Complex. Maybe a cook in the cafeteria. Maybe there was someone else whose bleary eyes I could meet who understood the displaced, dissociated feeling gnawing at me.

The scene I covered for the second act of *Mefistofele* took place in a scene set on a crooked mountaintop during the Witches' Sabbat, where witches and warlocks gather to pledge loyalty and obeisance to the Devil. As the energy mounts, his minions present him with a totem of the world, which Mefistofele crushes in his hands. "We dance, for the world is fallen," the ghouls cry out in orgiastic celebration. Behind the din, a spectral light beams from the rafters to reveal me, nude with a ring of blood around my neck, inside a castle tower. The Devil assures Faust, the protagonist, that I am some sort of illusion, but Faust realizes that I am real.

I was only assigned one client who gave me nightmares, and it was because he could not, allegedly, refrain from strangling his girlfriend. For the first time in my newfound anticarceral praxis, I faltered. Was this the first client of mine whom I could not advocate for? My supervisor reminded me that most people who are incarcerated will eventually get out, and that the trauma and violence of incarceration that grafts itself onto a person inside does not improve outcomes for that individual or the people in their life after release. Besides, she reminded me, no matter what happened, I was his advocate, not his girlfriend's, and it was not my role to presume that I knew what was best for all parties involved. For the first time, I understood the confused look on my classmates' faces. I wanted to be on the floor of a playroom with my legs in a wide V, doing after-school play therapy with toddlers. I wanted to compile hygiene kits for a women's shelter. I wanted to work with the sympathetic, the deserving. In the evenings, I watched Cristina, framed by the vanity mirror, giggling and gossiping as she drew a red neck ligature over her white body makeup. I remained her shadow, ready to step in if she got sick and the show needed its wounded apparition. At night, I dreamed of hands clasped around my neck, holding me down in bed while my capillaries burst and bloomed.

The mental health field uses the term "disenfranchised grief" to refer to the feelings of people mourning losses that are not acknowledged by our society. When I flip through textbooks and journal articles about disenfranchised grief, common examples are the feelings of loss upon the death of a pet, the death of a well-loved celebrity, or the many relocations of a military family. While we may understand that these things are sad, the allotment of sadness we ascribe to them is small and compartmentalized, and we may attempt to soothe by minimizing: *Just get another cat. You didn't even know them. You'll make friends at the new school.* Although these statements are often well-intentioned, they can teach people to stop talking about their pain, or maybe even to suppress their feelings altogether. But feelings vent like deep sea volcanic trenches. Whether they trickle out or explode, they have to come out somewhere.

Grieving over the anticipatory loss of our planet, grieving over the damage we are doing to our own species and others, grieving social inequality, these too are disenfranchised griefs, and they are nebulous and almost inconceivably vast. It is grief from which we are so disenfranchised that it's scarcely mentioned in the academic literature at all. I hear this kind of attenuation and disavowal time and again in people talking about their trauma: *Well, I don't have it as bad as some people.* This may very well be true. I cried into my yogurt because I have it so goddamn easy, and even that is hard.

Here's the thing, though. We don't grade our pain on a curve. You're allowed to feel sad about your gerbil dying, even if somewhere in the world, someone just lost their entire family. Pain is pain, and if we only let the person in the very worst circumstances feel it, then only one person in the world would be allowed to grieve on behalf of all of us—never-ending, unenviable work—and the rest of us would have to stuff our bubbling magma back underground.

We get to feel sad. While that may seem indulgent or selfish, paradoxically, feeling and working through our own grief grants other people space to feel theirs instead of looking around to ascertain the relative validity of their suffering. It also frees up room for us to care for others and to offer them things they might need to navigate their grief. Once pain is named, felt, and experienced, we may have a clearer understanding of how to move forward.

When I worked with my challenging client, I dug down as far as I could to the fundamental reasons for my advocacy. To contextualize my mitigation, I asked him about his childhood, the details of which I am required to hold in confidence but which I can assure you contain all of the jagged silhouettes of life-threatening terror. No one should have to grow up the way he did. When I could not feel empathy for the adult, I could imagine the child, a victim himself, who never got help and never felt heard. When I couldn't feel for him, I tried to imagine someone who could and to behave as they would. He hated me until the end of our work together, blaming me as the sole party responsible for his predicament. We had no miracle moments, no third-act revelations, no transformational allyship, and no favorable plea offer. One cannot be a social worker and expect only positive outcomes, even if it might make for a more inspirational story. He did leave me one lasting change, which was that I no longer read my clients' rap sheets before meeting them in person. To him I owe the belief that has paid dividends in my subsequent professional work: that we are more than who we are on our worst days. And I never went on stage to boil in the pot or to turn hauntingly in the tower. I remained a cover, a shadow, practicing in my head in case I was required to go on. I never actually made it to hell. Cristina was a professional, never late even once.

There is a comment on one of my burlesque videos online that says, "I'm super glad you guys can serve as ambassadors for all girls born with similar afflictions of the body and mind. You could also give to charity and read lol." The adage says don't feed the trolls, but I want to insert a gavage in this one. I want to feed and endlessly feed him with the things I am reading, the places I give to, what I do with my time when I'm not onstage, to inundate him with my bona fides. I want to stuff into him the futility I sometimes feel in the work that I do, the realization that the art I make might get mistaken for activism but that it's no substitute for a protest, a union drive, a letter delivered to a judge. I want to rebut him, but the work I do will never be enough. I'd love to know what cooldude6969* is doing with his time on Earth, but comparisons are rarely helpful for anything other than pettiness and temporary relief. My work is insufficient, and it is necessary. I will continue to know this, and it will continue to not be enough, and I will continue to sometimes fall short of an outcome that helps the people who are relying on me. Despite my best intentions, I will stumble into hypocrisy and use and misuse resources. I may always be a person who strives to do better and

---

*   Not his real name.

more and yet never does enough. I will always care and I will always be selfish. I move forward in this imperfectness.

I don't have what resembles a rigorous Jewish practice these days, especially not compared to my upbringing. What I choose to carry forward is an inalienable sense of belonging to the Jewish community, a sense of my inclusion in the diaspora, and *tikkun olam*, the imperative of repairing the world. Jewish people don't stress the afterlife so much, or at least if you asked a representative sample of different Jews, you would likely get several different answers, including some ineffectual shrugs. Stuff on Earth, we have opinions about. Ask whether pushing an elevator button counts as "work," and we can debate it for months. Ask about which animals we shouldn't eat, and we've got a comprehensive list. In my Hebrew school, I was taught how to pray, when to pray, what each holiday meant and how to celebrate it, how to live Jewishly, how to fear Jewishly, and even how to die Jewishly. We didn't talk so much about what came after that.

So here we are, alive and among alive people, people who deserve support, who deserve experiences that affirm their value and humanity. I am not awaiting a cosmic reward. I have already received it. I grew up with parents who made their love for me evident in their every action. I had people around who listened to me, who looked after me, who cultivated my interests and made room for my difference. I grew up white (or white enough, or white until, or white with an asterisk) and have received more than my fair share of the bounty of existence because of that, my yogurt with figs and honey. I was born into less struggle than any previous generation of my own family. The imperative to sow that gratitude into action on Earth is real. It sits on my chest. It keeps me from sleep. It is my rent to pay. It is my work. If not now, when?

I have completed my coursework and my internships. I no longer work in jails, but I continue to prefer work with populations our culture at large has deemed undeserving—sex workers, queer people, and trans people most especially. I wake up and read the news and freak all the way out and breathe and drink a cup of coffee and feed my cat. Then I sit in a room where my job is to be present for someone else, to meet them with whatever they are coming in with, and to give them a space to talk and be heard, to forge a way through the sludge of life. I find my empathy and dig down into it with grasping, grateful hands. We grieve losses and celebrate accomplishments, and I end my days worn out but full.

And, because I want to be a lot of things at once, I am still performing burlesque, because performing has become an indispensable part of my life. I wonder, sometimes, if I can continue to do this forever. I imagine combing my silver hair, turning over my desiccated old pasties in my papery hands, surrounded by the next generation of professionally naked people. What might that be like, to be an elder to someone, peeling apart stuck-together laminated pages of my scrapbook, pointing out my flyers from shows of decades past and cut-out newspaper clippings, flipping over yellowed business cards? Would anyone nod in reverence if I talked about the days of bringing a CD to the club? Something about aging in nightlife terrifies me. There are some models for it but none yet that is quite right for me. Still, it beats an early death or quitting this part of my existence that I love so much.

I've molded my life around my choice to remain in the low arts. I've sacrificed time, energy, money, stability, and sometimes my health and comfort to remain part of the lineup. If that decision means the different parts of my life coexist like spinning plates, each moving at the same time and in its own orbit, there will always be one wobbly one spinning out, needing more attention than it's getting, asking to be fixed or figured out or reconciled. Like any showman, I'm going to keep adding plates, because that makes for a better show. So I hope the tail of the comet of my existence will be long and dazzling, and I hope I can keep it all in the air. My time is precious and I have a lot to do.

And so, a prayer, for longevity and for my selves, and for the work to come: May the things I do always stem from gratitude. May I never forget my luck. May I have the wisdom to be fully awake and fully alive in whatever else happens to me. May I hurt as few and help as many as I can. May I outlive my self-doubt. May a beautiful world outlive me. May the work continue. Amen, amen, amen.

A Bag of Lube

. . . .

At the tail end of the summer season, the teeming swell of people waiting for corn dogs at the Surf Avenue Nathan's have thinned out to a single file, a faucet drip. It's quiet for the first time in months. The change of the season never feels as palpable as at the edge of the boardwalk, and the first weeks of September blow brisk breezes across the sand in the last pink streams of evening. The N, Q, D, and F trains slow down as they approach their terminuses, and the last five minutes of the aboveground subway commute squeaks around the bend in the tracks to reveal the neon spokes of the Wonder Wheel, the red peppermint bursts of the park entrance, the purple and blue arms of thrill rides and coasters that emerge from the night like sea monsters surfacing.

Outside of the busy season's beach bloat, the wide avenues outlining the shore feel suddenly deserted, and the multicolored marquees of Luna Park cast a lonesome smear into the surrounding darkness. After so many months of promising leisure and urging you to stop and look, Coney Island changes its tune in the fall, warning you to hurry to your destination, which in this case is a blessed two blocks from the train. A carnival barker in a straw-brim hat and sleeve garters opens the door into a lobby of several hundred people drinking, greeting each other with shrieks and kisses, shifting anxiously. A stage cat or dog darts through the room, activated by the energy. As showtime approaches, people tighten into a dense, thick queue by the theater entrance. A Coney Island USA employee announces that the house is open, his voice like a bullet from a starting pistol, and the crowd teems into the theater to find their seats, competing for the best vantage point for the Miss Coney Island Pageant.

They're right to throw elbows. The pageant is the highlight of the season. Contestants leave it all on the stage, having spent the year working in secret to craft acts, outfits, concepts, and gimmicks that will leave an indelible impression. And so, in any given year, you might see a performer with live goldfish swimming in her bra, someone tassel twirling with an eighteen-inch sword jammed down her throat, a contestant walking onstage wearing nothing but hot dogs held in place by plastic wrap, which plump and cook with her sweat and are served to the brave in the crowd. A gal who made her own costumes out of scraps and detritus has at least as good a chance as a competitor who spent thousands of dollars on a gown. People are there to be entertained and to see something they have never seen before.

The first Miss Coney Island Pageant was held in 2003 as a way to fill the end of the summer program at the hallowed, rickety Sideshows by the Seashore. The event was a remix of the boardwalk beauty pageants of the 1920s and 1930s, where pretty housewives flocked to have their legs evaluated for money and acclaim.

The 2003 pageant was a farce, and it was prescripted, rigged in favor of Bambi the Mermaid, an eccentric blonde sideshow queen and producer of *Burlesque at the Beach*, New York's oldest and longest continually running show of the neo-burlesque revival of the 1990s and 2000s.

The modern remix of Miss Coney Island is, like many byproducts of the burlesque revival, less concerned with proportions and poise and more focused on humor and spectacle. The first show was a hit and it continues to be the best attended event of the summer. Coney Island USA sells overflow seats so that people not lucky enough to snag a spot in the ass-smashing wooden theater bleachers can enjoy a live simulcast projected on a pull-down screen in the adjoining Freak Bar. It's the event of the season, right as the season ends.

Bambi herself selects ten performers to compete for the title, which confers personal bragging rights, accolades from other members of the scene, and a $100 bill taped onto an inflatable novelty item. During the pageant, the ten contestants must present their interpretation of evening wear, swimwear, and talent. The audience votes for the winner using golf pencils and paper ballots that are collected in glittery gift bags and hand counted. Over the years, as the number of burlesque performers in New York has increased, the competition has gotten more intense, and the mood has shifted from farcical to cutthroat, or at least a bit ruthless. And so in 2015—a full century after (as legend has it) a group of four recent immigrants settled a fearsome beachside debate about who among them was the most patriotic by engaging in the first Coney Island hot-dog-eating contest—I swallowed my fear and strapped myself to a refrigerator dolly for my first event: evening wear.

I was banking on a big first impression with the audience and I bet on two things: that my competitors were going to walk onto the stage for their presentation, and that they were going to dress up nicely. I made sure to do neither. I wore a dirty white American Apparel nightgown and a thrifted fencing helmet upon which I rhinestoned a pair of ghoulish red lips. Barefoot, I stepped onto a rusty hand truck, and a stagehand and I made sure I was strapped on tight with wraparound bungee cord. When my name was announced, the stagehand wheeled me on, my head obscured and heavy, lolling between my shoulders as if I were semiconscious. When I hit center stage, the kitten for the evening pulled off my helmet and slapped me in the face. I pretended to come to. "Did I win? Did I do good? Was I pretty?" I murmured. I attempted to raise a hand to greet the cheering crowd but settled for weak, ineffectual waving from under the cord.

While I gasped and sputtered onstage, Fredini, the night's emcee, read my bio:

> Fancy Feast has been naked her entire life but she has
> been putting glitter on her stretch marks professionally
> since 2011. She holds the title of Miss Bushwick
> Burlesque 2014. She has the dubious honor of having
> Coney Island reject one of her numbers because it was
> too much of a safety liability. This means a lot to her. Her
> platform is to have more women producers and MCs in
> burlesque, and she is passionate about destroying the

idea that only some kinds of bodies get to be sexy. If she wins Miss Coney Island, Fancy vows to make sure that the Coney Island sideshow feels accessible to its surrounding community and maintains a high standard for artistic excellence. If she loses she will slither back into the gutter where she came from.

The stagehand wheeled me off and untied me, and I rushed backstage to get ready for the talent portion of the evening. I was still feeling sick and feverish from a late-summer cold, and my skin felt clammy as I changed into the look with the help of Dolly Debutante, a juicy, get-shit-done femme who held a joint between her bubblegum-pink lips and zipped me up, unfettered by her stiletto manicure. With not a moment to spare, I was flagged to get back to the stage to perform, dressed in a gold floor-length sequin gown, a fluffy turkey-feather boa, and a green and pink feathered headdress with gold tassels, to which I nearly sacrificed my fingerprints in the Glue Gun Marathon of 2015. My talent portion began with a poem I'd written in the depths of my sickness and sleeplessness the night before, with stanzas like:

> I used to masturbate to stardom
> Startled into orgasm, a taste of what's to come
> But fat girls' dreams are whittled down like late night
>   infomercial waists
> We learn to waste away, the way uncertain
> I've stood behind this very curtain
> And curtailed dreams that there would be

*A crowd to see because I did not deserve the eyes to look
  at me*

The air was thick, warm, settled, quiet; I experienced the kind
of rapt attention that rarely happens in a room full of drunk people on a Friday night. The poem closed with a couplet introducing Katy Perry, and the first strains of her ode to empowerment,
"Firework," boomed out of the speakers. After a few seconds of
choreography, the audience could tell there was something different about the version I used. "Do you ever feel like a plastic bag,
like a plastic bag, like a plastic bag? Cause, baby, you're a plastic
bag, plastic bag, plastic bag, plastic bag, plastic bag . . ." I shed
my feather headdress and replaced it with one I had made of cat
food bags and take-out chopsticks. I tossed my boa and wrapped
myself in a long, variegated facsimile made of Key Foods grocery
bags. I zipped off my gown to reveal a full crinoline made of
more cat food bags, save for a gap around my butt where, upon
turning around, I revealed that I was wearing another bag like a
diaper, with a big red "THANK YOU" across the fanny. I took off
the skirt, then my plastic bra, revealing pasties fashioned from
different-size yellow smiley faces cut out of yet more plastic bags.
Then, as the song worked its way into the final crashing chorus,
I whipped off my underwear, pulled a plastic grocery bag out
of my vagina—into which I had poured a mixture of water and
organic water-based lubricant—shook it out so that it sprayed the
first three rows of the bleachers, and pulled the slimed contrap-
tion over my head and posed, breathing hard so the bag would
inflate and deflate with my respiration.

The song ended, and I held my pose to accept applause. When I took the bag off my head, the audience was on its feet for me (in the bar area with the simulcast as well, I was told). I gasped, aspirating lube.

My knees gave way the moment I stepped out of the stage light and I sat for a moment on the floor in exhaustion, over-whelmed. Then, a sip of water, a handful of almonds, and a more staid swimwear look: nude, but for a light blue and pearl mer-kin, pearl pasties, a waist-long wig, and an opalescent clamshell I'd made myself and wore like a backpack. Behind me I carried a diaphanous blue cloth that rippled like ocean waves. I was crowned Miss Coney Island 2016 just like that. A Fat Venus on the half shell.

It would be a mistake to believe that New York City has gentrified away the gritty glee and outsider art that called freaks of past generations to find a home here. If you believe that, it's because you hang out with boring people. Some things are harder to find now, as capitalism crunches over and prices out the communities that made New York a cultural hub, the wealth disparity and rampant greed in real estate meaning you can now buy a $900 pair of boots in the building that used to house the famed music venue CBGB, which itself hadn't been cool for some time. New Yorkers have felt the turnover grief of missing the hole-in-the-wall restaurant that got turned into a smoothie place that got turned into a Starbucks, and then even that got repurposed into a "luxury lifestyle environment" not accessible to the public, which must mean a venture capitalist wants to colonize another set of dreary greige rooms where he can film himself doing five-minute planks. Everything people say about New York is true; it's expensive, it's over, it's bullshit. And, to paraphrase Barbara Kingsolver, this is a city that eats itself and lives forever.

Fermenting in the rancid stomach of this place, away from the insipid risk-free appetites of corporate monoculture, I promise you that there are still places where you can pay $10 cash to the man at the door, get a stamp on your wrist, and sit next to strangers on a wooden bench while a sexy woman dressed as a chicken lays an actual egg and offers it to the audience. If we are to retain our very soul, we must tilt our faces and open our mouths to receive the gift. Filth is humanizing, nutritious. It reminds us of who we all are, who we try to pretend we aren't, everything about ourselves that we disavow and would rather push away.

Rose Wood, "the Mother of All Motherfuckers" and one of my great performance art heroes, once sat with me in a twenty-four-hour diner in the Lower East Side at dawn, little bits of makeup still clinging to her lips and smudging her napkin with lurid red as she ordered eggs with a soft kindergarten-teacher voice. Hours earlier, I'd watched Rose mesmerize an audience of terrible, rich cokeheads with her performance at the Box, an exclusive Nolita nightclub with a formidable reputation. Rose, who three hours before had been cutting her penis and shoving things in her ass and putting on lipstick in a mirror in front of two hundred people who had each paid $1,000 for bottle service. This is a woman whose stage performances are so extreme that the audience sometimes rushes the stage, their blood angry and churning, and then after the show, she walks home peppered with stares and transphobic harassment. This phoenix, who makes and unmakes herself on stage at 3 a.m., six nights a week, looked at my pale, clammy face as I sipped my tea and told me that not every performer gets to be a pretty princess. Most of the people who pay to see the show want to be the pretty princess themselves and are threatened by anyone else attempting to assume that role.

"Furthermore," she said, "people are deserving of their monsters. Your responsibility is not to turn people on, to be sexy for them. All you have to do is make them feel. They're desperate for it. Which is why all of my acts start with the same question: Where does it hurt?"

I nodded and felt a warm ache inside. *Oh Rose,* I thought, *it hurts everywhere.*

In the midst of my reigning year as Miss Coney Island, I began coproducing a show called *The Fuck You Revue* with my artistic partner, Zoe Ziegfeld, a former Coney Island snake enchantress, former club stripper, and former preschool teacher. She's also known as "the gal who puts the Bush in Bushwick," because she stopped shaving her bikini line years ago and has since let her politically trenchant thicket of pubes dwarf her G-strings like ivy reclaiming a historic building. Before we created the revue, we had moved in similar circles for years, and I admired her for her wit, goodness, impeccable taste, and unwillingness to compromise her values. We were both regular performers at a show Darlinda Just Darlinda produced called *Bushwick Burlesque,* and when the show closed after five years, we were offered their late-Tuesday-night time slot. The venue was a bar called Bizarre, which was owned by two French men of mixed renown and repute. They offered us the following deal: they would keep the money they made from the bar during showtime, less $100, which would go to Zoe and me. We would keep whatever money we could make at the door, although we weren't allowed to refuse entry to anyone who didn't feel like paying, so we had to call it a suggested donation. There were, the Frenchmen made sure to emphasize, no rules regarding content. We could do whatever we wanted, book whomever we wanted, and promotion would be up to us. We agreed. We had a show.

Bizarre itself was a bordello and brasserie, a dingy, low-lit den with ripped leather couches and flimsy wooden cabaret chairs; a warped, out-of-tune baby grand piano with a red-shaded lamp on it; and a stage area that was nothing more than a wooden box that bowed and splintered in the middle, painted black, with a repurposed church pew, instead of stairs, to use for stepping on and off. The cooks slung frites and Scotch eggs out of the kitchen, the bar featured an antique absinthe fountain with glowing green punch, and the downstairs bathrooms never contained all of the parts that comprised a complete working toilet. The whole place smelled right—like beer and cocaine and paint and dust.

The ethos of *The Fuck You Revue* was simple: we wanted to make a space for the edgier, weirder work our friends were making, the stuff that other producers passed on for any number of reasons. The wilder, the more political, the more troubling the act, the better. The stupider, the more tasteless, the more likely to be booked. Each *Fuck You Revue* would have a theme, Zoe and I decided. Our first show was a consecration that featured a lineup of just the two of us, each performing four acts, including one of each other's. Peter Aguero, a mahogany-voiced storyteller, emceed the show and officiated a wedding between the two of us; we were symbolically marrying as creative partners and committing ourselves to our work. The final number of the night was my performance of Zoe's cake-sitting act, and after the show she collected tips while I invited the audience to lick cake off my butt. We were able to pay our door girl, Qualms Galore, and our sound person, DJ Fresh Prince of Darkness, and still make a modest profit.

Convincing people to leave their houses to go to Bushwick at 10 p.m. on a Tuesday was a hard sell, so Zoe and I endeavored to make it the kind of show people would kick themselves for missing. Fortunately, even the most in-demand international burlesque talent could find themselves free on a Tuesday night, so Zoe and I were able to curate the lineups of our dreams, booking performers we'd admired as fans before our careers began, new performers with innovative concepts, and our contemporaries whose acts rocked boats and ruffled feathers elsewhere. Themes for our monthly production included a show where every act we booked broke a different law, back-to-back entries called "The Sex Show" and "The Unsex Show," and an annual celebration we called "Fucksgiving," a showcase of performers celebrating non-colonial-white-American cultures and heritages. Spurred by the excitement of creation and the fear that no one would show, Zoe and I became fierce, dogged production and promotion machines. Our fan base grew. Once all of the seats were claimed and the standing room got too tight in the back of the venue and along the bar, our audience began sitting on the floor in front of the stage like children at a library reading hour.

The shows were dirty, usually literally. Zoe cleaned the stage between acts wearing nothing but a garbage bag and combat boots, or sometimes just a diaper. Blood was spilled, sometimes on purpose and sometimes by accident. We had a piss protocol and an insertion protocol (you can do it but you're responsible for cleaning up what came out of you). Poison Eve once duck-walked across the uneven stage with each of her hands inserted into a whole raw chicken.* We booked an act that I couldn't watch without throwing up; a small price to pay—the number was that good (it involves cat food, but I don't want to spoil it for you). For Zoe's birthday one year, I dressed up and stripped as Gallagher and smashed a watermelon with a sledgehammer, lodging chunks of fruit in the ceiling and sound system. For my birthday, a performer did a handstand and put a lit candle in her vagina, and I blew it out while the audience sang "Happy Birthday."

Punctuating the profanity and mess was a kind of transcendence, the result of the intense mutual trust that developed over time with our regulars in the intimacy of that dank little bar. Darlinda Just Darlinda debuted an act where she imagined getting sick from a virus, making her way back to the stage one more time to dress up, strip, and die, which felt like far-off science fiction at the time. Glenn Marla performed with a puppet of his

---

* A vogue/ballroom dance step where the dancer drops into a squat and kicks their heels out as they move.

mother, telling stories of growing up in a fatphobic household. When a performer wanted to do an act without music, the audience did not need to be told how to hold the silence. An act about being a queer immigrant could be followed by an act with a stripping milkman that could be followed by a baton-twirling BDSM number that could be followed by a celebration of Juneteenth. Attendees were as likely to cry at the show as they were to laugh. Somehow it all fit. The audience just wanted to feel.

The Fuck You Revue became my favorite clock, the best way to tell time, to stretch toward something good at the end of a meaningless month. After the show was over, Zoe and I would sit on the dirty floor of the bar basement and fold stacks of cash into handwritten thank-you cards for our performers (that classy touch was all Zoe), gulping water from tall, sweaty glasses and marveling that we had pulled it off again.

The "You" of *The Fuck You Revue* was never our audience, despite our curtain call send-off ("Thank you for coming to the show, have a great night, and Fuck You!"). Rather, it was the whims of the amalgamated hetero-patriarchy that we raised our manicured middle fingers against. Even the burlesque community, which prides itself on being a bastion of outsiders, had begun pulling toward rewarding skinny cisgender white women who could drop thousands of dollars on professional costuming.

Think about it this way: Any marketed beauty ideal is designed to be unattainable, and it excludes people who are farther away from what makes safe, comfortable American money. A car show is not going to hire the performer who sticks a bottle of Jack Daniels up her ass, then takes a swig and sprays it into the crowd (Rose Wood, again). Neither is a luxury hotel going to hire a fat Black girl to be a costumed cigarette attendant. Both decisions are derived from the same phenomenon of "respectability" or "company image," but the former scenario may sting less than the second, because one is about artistic ethos and one is about identity. Choosing to exist outside of corporate virtue feels a hell of a lot better than having your choices made for you by the force of rejection.

Which is more obscene, really, a butthole or some unthinkable invention of late capitalism, like a $50 bottle of water? How extraordinary to make the mere reality of a body unacceptable, rather than the violence that is done to it by individuals and the state. The burlesque performers who have survived such violence find the abscesses of that cruelty inside of themselves, and many of them press into that hurt to make their art. Of course, it is the artistic reaction, not the harm, that is then reviled and legislated against, the mirror's reflection that is hated rather than the object itself. So we exaggerate the reflection, magnify it until it becomes an archetype, a symbol, something more easily communicated and digested. Rose Wood in my head says, *People are deserving of their monsters.*

After all, the best stories are the ones scribbled in marginalia. And that's why we perform pressed into the hemline between city and sea, in the hours just before dawn, in the gray area of legality and the blurring of gender and respectability, discarded people making art from discarded things. It is in this inhospitable terrain that we root like pioneer plants, drawing sustenance from crumbling rock, hugging coastline, and knowing that we could be obliterated by a rising tide. Maybe that sounds too dreamy, but it is down here in the muck that I feel romantic.

On the night the new winner was crowned, I left the Miss Coney Island pageant with my legacy: a new tradition of a step-down number from the previous queen, to cover the uneasy minutes after the show when bags of ballots are upended onto a white plastic table in the Coney Island gift shop and counted, and the audience shifts around impatiently for the results. So why not have one last hurrah for the outgoing queen? At the end of my year as Miss Coney Island, in fall 2016, I took the stage in my crown and sash, dressed in royal purple. First I stripped out of the crown, then the sash, and when my dress wouldn't fit over my head, I popped off my big black beehive wig, which cut nine inches off my height. I took off my dress like a child might, clumsily, crouching down to the floor to step out of it, revealing a regular set of bra and panties. In the span of ninety seconds, I had reduced myself from title holder to a plain nothing. The bra came off, then the panties, then with a heaving sigh, I opened my legs and pulled out another plastic bag—once more with feeling. Into the bag, I stuffed my sash and my crown. I plucked a wooden dowel from the floor and tied the bag into a bindle stiff, which I popped over my shoulder as I mimed trying and failing to hitchhike, watching with growing concern as I imagined cars streaking past me, naked in my heels on a stretch of lonesome highway. My friend Max Vernon joined me on stage; they had written a perfect song called "Lower East Side Angry Face," which they played live as I stripped. The song closes with these lyrics:

Now it's someone else's chance
To be photographed nightly in thrifted couture
Feel rock bottom sadness the drugs cannot cure
My brain is Swiss cheese and the past is a blur
But once upon a time I knew what my best angles were
I knew what my best angles were

Thus concluded my reign: ignored by the imaginary motorists for whom I held no allure, my title and the trappings of my grandiosity stripped away, leaving nothing but a washed-up civilian, the fickle tides of audience attention having ebbed. Showbiz is always dying, venues are closing, and everyone is nostalgic for the way it was, or never was, or should have been. And in the endings there are beginnings. You leave the stage and someone is next in the lineup after you, getting ready to begin. A girl steps forward into a spotlight. Six feet away from her, an audience member lifts their head to bask in the reflection of stage lights on rhinestones for the very first time. The cultural earthworms who digest pain and make art are constructing sand castles in the trash-flecked sands of Coney Island. As things fall apart around us, we may as well build something to remember.

ACKNOWLEDGMENTS

This book would not exist without the expertise and perseverance of my literary agent, Connor Goldsmith. He saw the book first, before I did. Connor fought for this project with a kind of tenacity I would not expect from even the most unrelenting advocates, including taking conference calls from a hospital bed—several times, if memory serves—and talking me off a ledge over chicken tenders at the slowest diner in Brooklyn through a year and a half on submission. He told me he kept pushing because he did not like being wrong. Connor, I hope I proved you right.

I brought my editor Abby Muller a bucket of loam, and she envisioned a clay vessel. I cannot thank her enough for providing the vision that constructed the purpose behind my stories. Abby is a master builder of narrative intention, but she is more than a sensational editor. Her warm, precise feedback and encouragement has changed the way I relate to the events of my own life that are contained within this book; it's not just the book but my life that is richer for it.

I am indebted to my editors Mae Zhang McCauley and Maddie Jones, who embraced this project with warmth and zeal at a pivotal time in its development. I am grateful to have seen the book through with such a bright and indefatigable team. I did not earn their wisdom or favor through my incoherent e-mail brainstorms, and yet there it was for me in abundance.

Bless the creative team at Algonquin for facilitating the publishing of all this good filth. Thank you to everyone at Hachette who inherited it with open arms. Christopher, thank you, especially, for your design work, and for waiting for me in the cold to hand off a bucket of my pasties for the cover image.

Thanks to the fine people at Fuse Literary for their patience, guidance, and good advice as I baby-deer-walked through the process of becoming a first-time author. I didn't know what I didn't know, and now I know, thanks to them.

I salute Jenna Johnson, whose insight and edits shaped one of my favorite essays in the bunch and gave me the hope that this was a project with legs. Thank you to Leon Chase and Rachel Sanders for opening doors in my career at pivotal moments. Thank you to Stoya and Sweetpea, and the ZeroSpaces team, for their help developing what turned into "Doing Yourself."

I cribbed the word *wormwend* from @actualperson084 on Twitter; it's a great one.

I am in awe of my deep bench of generous friends. I am indebted to Sam Sax, Jo Weldon, and Shelby Lorman, for their industry insight and commiseration. Thank you to Robert McVey, for his pith and vinegar; Dain, Brant, Porcelain, Evelyn, and Tiger, for their close listening and excellent feedback. Thank you to Emily, Zoe, Tim, Laura, Arielle, Eric, Micheal, Alex, Iris, Amanda, Aisha, Max, and Rishi for their love and faith, for letting me prattle on about book news, and for attending shows and continuing to check in on me despite the rapidly diminishing returns of asking me how the writing was going. Jamal, your love is the kind that feeds me like bread and butter. To the members of RWDSU's Dildos United, and to my burlesque contemporaries and predecessors who have informed this book from the inside out with their art, thank you for crossing paths with me and giving my life texture and meaning.

I'm so grateful for my family, whose intense, unrelenting love and encouragement of my individuation imperative has allowed me to venture far and know that someone will have my back. It is their standard for my work that I write to, regardless of subject matter. Thank you for always making room for who I am. I love you to the wildest depths of me.

I must acknowledge the locations where this book was written over the course of five years: first in the Babeland LES basement, between the hot pipe and the fly strips; at the West Brooklyn; in the supernumerary dressing room at the Metropolitan Opera; in the backseat of Evelyn DeVere's car; in the hallways of the Silberman School of Social Work; at Chez V in Greenport; at Deck Feeling on the island of Syros; and most importantly, in my bed, where all my best work is conceived.

NOTE ON SOURCES

. . . .

The internet was a great friend as I cobbled together events and fact-checked them to the best of my ability. Some of my external research is cited directly in text, and my other sources are listed below.

Information about Pinchbottom Burlesque came from their own website and archived issues of the *Village Voice*. Scholarship about SESTA/FOSTA was sourced from Hacking // Hustling and Survivors Against SESTA, and from the collective knowledge of sex-worker Twitter. Information about the Blue Laws in Tennessee is courtesy of the producers of the Nashville Burlesque Festival, as well as an article in *Pin Curl Magazine*. Minimum wage and cost of living statistics are from CBS News and the Guttmacher Institute. Details about butterfly metamorphosis were cribbed from *Scientific American*. I double-checked my ancestral knowledge of Jewish housewarming traditions with those that were published in the *Chicago Jewish News*. Information about Coney Island history came from a website erroneously named Stuff Nobody Cares About, and from the Coney Island USA website.

Where possible, I consulted many of the parties mentioned or involved to check for accuracy and obtain permission for inclusion. Some names have been changed to protect individuals' privacy.